Also by Robin Ulbredtch

HEART to heart: A Discipleship and Mentoring Plan

Behold Our Awesome God!

A HEART to heart Bible Study

Robin Ulbredtch

WESTBOW®
PRESS
A DIVISION OF THOMAS NELSON
& ZONDERVAN

Unless otherwise noted:

Scripture taken from the New King James Version.**
Copyright 1982 by Thomas Nelson, Inc.
Used by permission. All rights reserved.

**Scripture source is the NKJV Study Bible
If listed in the Bibliography would be:
Radmacher, Earl D., ed. NKJV Study Bible, 2nd Edition, Nashville,
TN: Thomas Nelson, Inc., 1997, 2007, pp. throughout.

WestBow Press books may be ordered through booksellers or by contacting:

WestBow Press
A Division of Thomas Nelson & Zondervan
1663 Liberty Drive
Bloomington, IN 47403
www.westbowpress.com
1 (866) 928-1240

ISBN: 978-1-4908-6933-9 (sc)
ISBN: 978-1-4908-6935-3 (hc)
ISBN: 978-1-4908-6934-6 (e)

Library of Congress Control Number: 2015902108

Printer information available on the last page.

WestBow Press rev. date: 03/05/2015

Dedication

This book is dedicated to:

Jesus, my Savior and Lord, for paying the price for my sins, for saving me, and for the wonderful things He does in my life.

Steve, my husband, for his patience and assistance in helping make this dream become a reality.

Pastor Wesley Ribeiro, the Elders, Deacons, and their wives, from Sandpoint Christian Center, who counseled, encouraged, and spurred me on to do what God has asked of me. They encouraged me to step out in the faith, to believe, and to fulfill the vision God has given me.

Leitha Harvey, for believing in me, helping, and standing beside me. I wish to thank Leitha for her many encouraging words that spurred me on to write, and for her great example of a godly woman. I pray that I can encourage and be a godly example for others, as she has been for me.

All the brothers and sisters in Christ who have encouraged and prayed for me over the years.

C. Max and Gail Kalben for their encouragement and prayers for me over the years as I helped and interacted with them at Bonner Gospel Mission.

Nils Rosdahl, my former Journalism Instructor from North Idaho College in Coeur d' Alene, Idaho, for taking his time and dedicating his life to teaching me and many other students how to write.

May God bless you all!

Contents

Preface

"I will extol You, my God, O King,
and I will bless Your Name forever and ever.
Every day I will bless You,
and I will praise Your name forever and ever.
Great is the Lord, and greatly to be praised;
and His greatness is unsearchable.
One generation shall praise Your works to another,
and shall declare Your mighty acts.
I will meditate on the glorious splendor of Your majesty,
and Your wondrous works.
Men shall speak of the might of Your awesome acts,
and I will declare Your greatness."
--Psalm 145:1-6

Before the foundations of the world, God knew me. He created me and led me down the path of life, eventually drawing me into His loving arms. This journey began even before my birth on December 26, 1956, in a small rural hospital in Bonners Ferry, Idaho.

During my preschool years my family lived in Moyie Springs, a small village about ten miles from Bonners Ferry. Here God began drawing me down the path He had prepared for me. One day a friend, whose identity I don't recall, took me to services at that small church in Moyie Springs. During church someone gave me a little children's Bible with a pink imitation-leather cover, gold-edged pages, and a few pictures, including one of Jesus hanging on the cross at Calvary.

As I remember, this was my first encounter with God's Word, the Holy Bible, yet somehow I knew this was a special book. From that day on babysitters and others read that Bible to me. As a result, I came to know the most precious gift of all—Jesus—who is revealed in its pages. The Bible is His story. He alone has power to change, heal, and save lives!

I kept that Bible until the 1990's when two little girls passed through my life. These elementary-age girls were poor, and their family lived in the back of a pickup truck in the middle of the snowy winter. They had few possessions and little hope. So I gave them the pink Bible, along with some other Christian children's books, and prayed God would help them, and draw them to Himself as He had done for me. Those girls have never reentered my life, but I know God is with them, drawing them, and watching over their lives, because He answers prayer!

God showed me how awesome He is when He miraculously stopped me from ending my life. He revealed the truth of His unconditional love for me when I thought my life was worthless and hopeless. God transformed my broken heart and life, and made me a new creation in Christ Jesus! He brought me out of a life of depression and sin, and gave me a new life filled with forgiveness, love, joy, peace, and hope. He also gave me many blessings and promises for the future. As Scripture says, "I waited patiently for the LORD; and He inclined to me, and heard my cry. He also brought me up out of a horrible pit, out of the miry clay, and set my feet upon a rock, and established my steps. He put a new song in my mouth—praise to our God: many shall see it, and fear, and will trust in the LORD." (Psalm 40:1-3)

Because of God's divine intervention in my personal life, I am alive today to testify that God has done a marvelous work in my life! He has healed me from many wounds, and now He uses me as His instrument to take the wonderful news of His forgiveness and grace to others. Only God can take a broken life, restore it, and bring something good out of it that will benefit others. Behold, our awesome God!

As you work through this Bible study, I believe and pray that God will use it to draw people, teach His word, reveal His unconditional love, and reveal Himself to you. I also pray that you will let God heal and transform your life too!

This teaching is my way of saying, "Thank You, awesome God, for saving me, transforming my life, and giving me hope for the future!"

"To God be the glory!"

Welcome!

Welcome to 'Behold Our Awesome God!' the first in a series of personal Bible Studies that God has put on my heart to write. Preparing this study has been a blessing and a joy! I hope you enjoy working through it as much as I enjoyed preparing it.

This is a 13-week personal Bible study on the attributes and works of God, and how He works in the lives of people. It's my goal that these lessons will teach and encourage you to dig deeper into God's word and to get to know Him better.

These Bible study lessons can also be used for group studies. For further information, see my previous book called *HEART to heart: A Discipleship and Mentoring Plan,* as it is filled with valuable information about leading group Bible studies. Also, in the back of this book, I prepared a section called the Teacher-Leader's Guide which includes information to help you teach the lessons in this book.

If you have not accepted Jesus Christ as your personal Savior, He is standing at the door of your heart, waiting, and wanting you to open it and invite Him in. Scripture tells us, "For God so loved the world that He gave His only begotten Son, that whoever believes in Him should not perish but have everlasting life. For God did not send His Son into the world to condemn the world, but that the world through Him might be saved." (John 3:16-17) God doesn't want people to go to hell, but He doesn't want to force them to love Him either. Therefore, He gave us each a choice, and we choose where we will spend eternity: Heaven or Hell. Our choice must be made with a sincere heart.

For those who sincerely recognize their need for God, a Savior to help them in life, only three small steps need to be taken before they can belong to the kingdom of God. First, the person must recognize they are a sinner, in need of God's forgiveness. Second, they need to ask God to forgive them for all of their sins. Finally, they need to talk to God (pray), and ask Jesus to come and live in their heart, and become their Lord and Savior.

As your guide through these lessons, I do not know where you stand. Therefore, I can only tell you about the choices, and your decision is between you and God. However, if you decide to accept Jesus Christ and take the steps above, please let me know by emailing me at getrobinu@gmail.com You need to be connected to a local church family so you can grow, learn more about God, and experience fellowship with other believers. Also, at some time in your life, you may need to get counsel or advice from a good pastor or church leader to help you as you walk with God. I would like to congratulate, encourage, and pray for you! In addition, if you have any questions or comments about this Bible study, you can email me at the above address and I will do my best to answer them.

For those who accept Jesus as their personal Savior, Ephesians 2:19-22 says, "Now, therefore, you are no longer strangers and foreigners, but fellow citizens with the saints and members of the household of God, in whom you are also being built together for a dwelling place of God in the Spirit."

God uses His Word to build His spiritual house. God's powerful, living Word brings people out of darkness and into the light. This change begins to take place when we are born again (ask God to forgive us for our sins and invite Jesus to come and live in our hearts).

New birth (or being born again) is a spiritual work, done by the Holy Spirit, in our hearts, as we choose to accept Jesus Christ. (See John chapter 3) As we believe and walk in the light of God's Word, He transforms us.

God's Holy Spirit, who lives in believers' hearts, shows us the true meaning of spiritual things. Without Him living in us, we cannot understand Spiritual things. Therefore, studying and comprehending the truth of God's word is difficult.

For those who believe in Jesus Christ and the work He did on the cross at Calvary, God has a mighty, everlasting plan for our lives. God chose us to be His children, and provides a great inheritance for us in heaven. In 1 Peter 2:9 scripture tells us, "But you are a chosen generation, a royal priesthood, a holy nation, His own special people, that you may proclaim the praises of Him who called you out of darkness into His marvelous light."

We will begin our Bible study at the beginning—with God—because He is the Divine One who was in the beginning, and who plans, designs, and orchestrates all of the building and sustaining of God's kingdom, and His heavenly household.

In this study we will behold examples of God's character, power, and works. As we explore God's Word, it's my hope that you will see and understand why God is so awesome, and if you haven't already, you will make a personal decision to love Him, and let Him be your God too!

For those already in God's family, this study will refresh your memory about God, increase your knowledge of Him, and hopefully expand your personal perception of His divine being. God is always bigger than we perceive Him to be because our human minds cannot conceive or fully understand His being or His ways!

Remember, you are not alone on the journey through this Bible study. The God who created the universe is with you, and He will reveal Himself to you, help you get to know Him better, and do amazing things in your heart and life! I will also be praying that God will do mighty things, and that you will come to know Him better! May God bless you mightily as you study His Word and 'Behold Our Awesome God!'

Introduction

As we 'Behold Our Awesome God,' we will learn about His character traits, divine activities, and powerful intervention in the lives of His people. We will see Him in action, and through His actions come to see how awesome He is. We will see the movement of God in the lives of people in the Bible, and in our own hearts and lives as well. We can learn a great deal about God from His written word, The Holy Bible. But no man, except for Moses (See Exodus 33:11), has ever seen God face to face. So when I say, "Behold Our Awesome God," we behold Him through the written Word, what we learn, and our personal encounters with the Holy Spirit during our prayer and personal-relationship times with Him. As you will learn later, God is an invisible but powerful being!

God is more powerful and more loving than you and I can ever search out and understand. Our human minds simply cannot fathom the greatness of God. In Psalm 145:3 King David wrote, "Great is the Lord and most worthy of praise; His greatness no one can fathom." King Solomon, the wisest man ever to live, wrote, "He has made everything beautiful in its time. He has also set eternity in the hearts of men; yet they cannot fathom what God has done from beginning to end." (Ecclesiastes 3:11) The Apostle Paul wrote, "Now we see but a poor reflection as in a mirror; then we shall see face to face. Now I know in part; then I shall know fully, even as I am fully known." (1 Corinthians 13:12) The scripture tells us that we cannot fully understand God but we can learn nuggets of truth about Him from His word, and He reveals Himself to His children as they seek to know Him by entering into a personal one-on-one relationship with Him through prayer and reading His word.

Even though evidence of God's existence surrounds us in creation, somehow some people convince themselves that God doesn't exist or they don't need Him. Nothing is farther from the truth! If people would truly cry out to God and walk in relationship with Him, they would come to realize that a relationship with the living God, Yahweh, is vital and exciting! Each step we take with God brings new adventure and challenges us to exercise our faith, and trust Him with our lives. God is big and powerful enough to take care of us—if we would only let Him.

Scripture tells us, "For since the creation of the world His invisible attributes are clearly seen, being understood by the things that are made, even His eternal power and Godhead, so that they are without excuse." (Romans 1:20). Yet sometimes, with our busy schedules, we don't stop to take the time to explore or truly see the evidence of God's character or His invisible qualities in the world around us. If we would stop and intensely look at even the smallest parts of creation—and be truthful with ourselves—we would have to admit that there is an awesome creator who made everything and sustains it. (Colossians 1:15-17)

For example, let's consider the raindrops. God's perfectly planned and synchronized design appears in the shape and pathways of the raindrops that fall from the sky. As each droplet falls, it has a unique path to follow, watering and sustaining life all along its way, until it reaches its final destination in a lake, river, creek, pond or ocean. When the raindrop reaches its final destination (if not before) the sun comes out and it evaporates into the air. Then the wind carries it across the land, and it eventually comes down to the earth to begin another life-sustaining journey. This 'cycle of the raindrops' could not have happened by chance because it is so perfectly synchronized to sustain life on this earthly creation.

Raindrops, as they travel their life-sustaining journey, also provide great natural beauty on the earth. They sustain all of the vegetation and create waterways, where wildlife and birds gather to get their life-sustaining water. The wildlife and waterways, with their rich colors and wide variety of forms, enhance the world around them and provide great natural wonders and beauties for the onlooker to see.

We can also see God's handiwork in the heavens as we look up on a dark night. We can see the moon and stars, which seem to keep their place, without falling down on us. They light up the night sky, declaring God's invisible greatness!

Furthermore, with new technology such as powerful man-made telescopes and satellites, we can now photograph portions of the universe. From these photographs we can again see God's perfectly synchronized creation in the location and orbit of the planets around the sun. Our planet earth was placed in heaven, in the exact location and orbit where it can keep the correct temperature and atmosphere for sustaining life on the planet. Colossians 1:17 says, "And He is before all things, and in Him all things consist." Behold, our awesome God is the super glue that holds everything together!

It is impossible for mankind to originate even one minute part of creation or sustain it. This unfathomable creator and sustainer of life is the one true God who expresses Himself in three persons: God the Father, God the Holy Spirit, and God the Word and Son, Jesus. Together they make up the One and Only true God. Just look around you, and look closely at the smallest parts of creation, and you will see the handiwork of God. Behold, our awesome God!

Without God there is no hope, love, meaning, purpose or lasting reward in this life or in eternity. Only God can provide these things for us. So let's forge ahead and look at the source of eternal treasure. May God get the glory for all He has done, is doing, and will do in the future!

Lesson 1

God Is Awesome!

"The Lord reigns; let the people tremble!
He dwells between the cherubim;
Let the earth be moved!
The Lord is great in Zion, and He
is high above all the peoples.
Let them praise Your great and awesome name—
He is holy."
--Psalm 99:1-3

"For the Lord Most High is awesome;
He is a great King over all the earth."
--Psalm 47:2

Open in Prayer

Prayer is simply talking to God and sharing what's on your heart and mind with Him. It's a relationship between the two of you. There is not a set procedure for prayer, and it doesn't have to be fancy or long. Just take a moment to ask God to help you get to know Him, and to show you how awesome He is. Spend a few minutes each day speaking to God and reading His Word.

Memory Verses

Take a few minutes each day to memorize the opening verses. They will reassure you whenever you go through difficult times, because they remind us of God's love, power, and ability to help and keep us. God will never forsake or leave His children!

Beginning Activity: Your Personal Journal

In the back of this book you will find blank personal journal pages to use for completing this activity and others in the lessons to come. For this activity, think about and list some facts you already know about God's character, power, and work. If you're a new believer, list some things you've heard about God or perhaps you have some questions you would like answered. Write your list in the journal and set it aside for future reference. When you are done, move ahead to the lesson introduction.

Lesson Introduction

In this lesson we see how God displays His awesome power to people living in Old Testament times.

God's Word tells us, "Every good gift and every perfect gift is from above, and comes down from the Father of lights, with whom there is no variation or shadow of turning" (James 1:17). God's Word is a good, perfect, and eternal gift He has given to us. From His Word we can learn about Him, the wonderful things He has prepared for those who believe in His Son, Jesus, and the work Jesus accomplished on the cross at Calvary.

God does not lie or change His overall plans like people do, because God does not change. God will continue working, and displaying His power among the peoples of the earth, until His plan is completed.

As we study Scripture, we see that God—also named Yahweh, the God of Israel—is the only true, living God. Though people worship other people, places, ideas or objects, the truth is—these can never be true gods.

In this week's lesson we learn about an earthly king named Nebuchadnezzar, who tries to force his subjects to bow down and worship a large gold image he had made. The king tries to force three of God's people to bow down and worship the gold image too.

The God of Israel commands His people not to worship any false gods or false idols. He is the only true God, and He is jealous for His people. So let's read about King Nebuchadnezzar and his image of gold, and find out what happened to God's people.

In the Word

Read Daniel chapter 3 and then move forward to complete the rest of the lesson.

Questions to Consider

1. What did King Nebuchadnezzar request the people in his provinces do?

2. Why did the three Jewish men refuse to obey the king?

3. What happened to the men when they refused to obey the king's order?

4. What miracle took place when the three men were in the furnace?

5. In the end, what did King Nebuchadnezzar say about the God of Shadrack, Meschack and Abed-Nego?

The answers to the Questions to Consider segment, for this lesson and those following, are located in the section called "Awesome Answers" in the back of this book. If you have trouble figuring out the answers, you can locate them in the book and learn from them.

Please try finding the answers in the Scripture before looking at the answers. By searching through Scripture, you will learn and retain more of the text, and you will be blessed!

Journal Activity

For your journal activity choose one of the following items to write about:

1. Spend some time meditating on this lesson. List some of God's character traits you noticed in this true story. Write these down in your journal. Also note in your journal any thoughts, ideas, or special words you received from God.

2. Imagine you were one of the onlookers in this crowd of officials. What would you think if you had seen this miracle happen before your eyes? Would this convince you the God of Shadrack, Meschack, and Abed-Nego is real? Write down any thoughts you might have about this miraculous work of God. Also write down any personal experiences or anything else God brings to your mind, such as a Bible verse, idea, story to share, or any questions you may want to bring up.

3. Imagine you are in the same situation as the three Jewish men. What would you feel inside? How would you like being in front of a crowd and having a king asking you questions about your God? Would you go along with the crowd or would you go against the flow? What would God want you to do? Do you think God would be there to help you in this trial? Write a paragraph about your thoughts on your journal page for this lesson. Be careful not to let the enemy put a guilt trip on you if you think you would fall because of the peer pressure. Many of us have a difficult time standing firm in the faith during great trials.

Decisions for Life

In this lesson you read about how the God of Shadrack, Meshack, and Abed-Nego saved His servants from an angry king and his fiery furnace. God proved to these people that He is real and powerful. He has the ability and the power to take care of His servants!

You also saw an example of someone setting up a false god. Frequently people set up other people, places, things, ideas, or activities as false gods or idols in their lives. As Christians, we need to continually check our hearts to see if we have any false gods or idols in our lives. If we find something that we've set up as an idol, we need to compare it to the one true God, the God of Shadrack, Meshack, and Abed-Nego, and decide which one we are going to serve. Then we need to put God in His proper place in our lives—as our first priority. If God isn't in His proper place in your life, I challenge you to make the decision to correct the situation, and make your relationship with Him your first priority.

In the story of Joshua in the Old Testament, he brought people to the point of making decisions in their lives by saying,

—Now therefore, fear the Lord, serve Him in sincerity and in truth, and put away the gods which your fathers served on the other side of the River and in Egypt. Serve the Lord! And if it seems evil to you to serve the Lord, choose for yourselves this day whom you will serve (...). But as for me and my house, we will serve the Lord— (Joshua 24:14-15)

I challenge you to consider what Joshua said, and make a decision as to whom you will serve. Make a decision for your life, and stand firm in it! If you haven't already, I pray you will choose to serve the one true, living God.

Live the Life

As Christians we need not only learn the Word of God, but also need to learn how to put the things we've learned into practice in our lives. Choose one of the following activities and apply what you've learned from this lesson to your daily life:

1. Do you have a personal testimony of a time when God rescued you from trouble? Do you believe God is big enough to take care of you? If so, why? Write down your testimony and personal thoughts on your journal page for this lesson. Then pray, and thank God for what He did.

2. Reflect on your life, and think about an awesome work God has done for you. Ask God for the courage and boldness to tell others about what God's done for you and how awesome He is. Then share your testimony with someone who needs encouragement.

3. Reflect and consider the priorities in your life. If you have placed something in your life as more important than God,

repent and get God back in His rightful place. Then endeavor to keep Him first on your list of priorities.

Review, Reflect, and Respond

Spend some time reviewing this lesson. Then write a paragraph or list the things you learned this week. As you study more about God in the upcoming lessons, add the new things you learn to your list. Periodically review your list or paragraph to remind you of how big and powerful God is, and that He can take care of you.

Close in Prayer

Pray and thank God for His love and protection. Ask God to reveal Himself to you. Also ask God what He would have you do in response to this lesson.

Lesson 2

God Is the All-Sufficient One

"Come and see the works of God;
He is awesome in His doing
toward the sons of men."
--Psalm 66:5

"O God, You are more awesome than Your holy places.
The God of Israel is He who gives
strength and power to His people.
Blessed be God!"
--Psalm 68:35

"And my God shall supply all your need
according to His riches in glory
by Christ Jesus."
--Philippians 4:19

Open in Prayer

During your prayer time this week ask God to demonstrate His all-sufficiency to you, and how He works through His people to get His work done. Try to spend a few minutes each day talking to God, and reading His word. Makes notes in your journal of any times you see God working through His people.

Memory Verses

Spend some time each day this week planting the memory verses for this lesson in your heart and mind. They will encourage you as you build your personal relationship with God.

Beginning Activity

Take a few minutes and consider your relationship with God. Can you remember a time when God provided for you, or used you to touch someone else's life? Write a paragraph in your journal describing what happened. Then move forward to the lesson introduction.

Lesson Introduction

In this lesson we will see one example of how God works through His people to do His awesome works. In this example, God works through His prophet Elijah to perform some miracles.

Though some people believe God doesn't do miracles today, this is a false teaching. God's word tells us God doesn't change. In scripture it says, "For I am the Lord, I do not change; therefore you are not consumed, O sons of Jacob."(Malachi 3:6) It also says, "Every good gift and every perfect gift is from above, and comes down from the Father of lights, with whom there is no variation or shadow of turning." (James 1:17) Job speaks of God's unchanging qualities when he says, "But He [God] is unique, and who can make Him change? And whatever His soul desires, that He does." (Job 23:13)

Miracles are all around us! Each time a baby is born, that is a new miracle from God! Every time someone is healed from sickness—that is a miracle as well. Perhaps you've had a financial crisis and lacked food, when suddenly, out of an unexpected source, a check arrived in the mail to meet your need. God works miracles to make sure His people have provisions. Also, God has given the gift of "working miracles" to some of His children, and He works through them to provide miracles to those around them.

Scripture tells us there are various gifts God gives to His children. Each one gets a unique set of gifts, depending upon what God chooses for that child. "But the manifestation of the Spirit is given to each one for the profit of all; for to one is given the word of wisdom (...), to another the word of knowledge (...), to another faith (...), to another gifts of healing (...), to another the working of miracles, to another discerning of spirits, to another different kinds of tongues, to another the interpretation of tongues. But one and the same Spirit works all these things, distributing to each one individually as He wills." (1 Corinthians 12:7-11)

God also gives us His reason for giving these gifts in 1 Corinthians 12:7 (quoted above): for the profit of all God's children. Scripture also gives us another reason for God's working of miracles, saying, "And they went out and preached everywhere, the Lord working with them and confirming the Word through the accompanying signs. Amen." (Mark 16:20)

Since God does not change, and the Gospel of Mark tells us that miracles confirm the preaching of God's word, we can know God still gives gifts, including the gift of working of miracles, to His children, and He still uses them to confirm the preaching of His word.

In our time in the Word this week we will see how God uses His servant to accomplish His awesome work.

In the Word

For this week's lesson read 1 Kings, chapter 17.

Questions to Consider

1. Where did the Lord tell Elijah to go after the prophet delivered the message of drought to King Ahab?

2. How did the Lord arrange for Elijah to have food to eat while he stayed in this place?

3. When the brook ran dry, who did God send Elijah to see so He could provide for the needs of His people?

4. How did God provide for the needs of these people during Elijah's stay in Zarephath?

5. What miraculous work did God use Elijah to do for the widow's son that inspired the woman to say, "Now by this I know that you are a man of God, and that the word of the Lord in your mouth is the truth?"

Journal Activity

After reading the true stories presented in this lesson, choose one of the following questions and write a paragraph in response to it on your journal page for this lesson:

1. If you were in Elijah's place and watched your food being brought to you by ravens, what thoughts do you think would be going through your mind?

2. If you were in Elijah's place and had to tell evil King Ahab the Lord was sending a drought to his kingdom, how would you feel about delivering this message?

3. If you were the woman from Zarephath, and you had only enough food to make one last meal, how would you feel about sharing the meal with a stranger?

4. If you were the woman at Zarephath, and you saw your flour and oil were not being used up even though you fed the prophet and your family from it, how would you respond to the Lord's working of this miracle right before your eyes?

5. How do you think the two stories in this lesson show us that God is a loving, personal God who knows and cares for each of His people?

Remembering the times God provided for us in the past encourages us to trust Him for our future provision. God CAN and WILL take care of His children's needs!

In Matthew 6:25-34 Jesus, God's Son, instructs us not to worry about our provision of food and clothing because He feeds the sparrows, and clothes the lilies of the field, and we are more valuable than they. Instead of worrying, He tells us to "seek first His kingdom and His righteousness," and all these things will be given to us as well. He also encourages us not to worry about tomorrow, for tomorrow will worry about itself. Each day has enough trouble of its own.

For many of us, worry is a challenge. It's hard to trust when you don't see the answer coming, or see how it could happen. Yet God is always faithful to take care of His children!

Decisions for Life

In this lesson we've learned about how well God takes care of His people. As the world grows more spiritually dark, and the prices on food and other needs keep rising, it's easy to get our eyes on the circumstances, and begin worrying. At times we even doubt God's ability and desire to take care of us. So make a decision to trust God more, and give your worries to Him in prayer. Then stand back and watch, as God shows you how well He can provide for your needs.

Now note I said "needs" not "wants." Though God will give us the desires of our hearts—if it's in His will—He does not promise to give us all of our wants. At times the things we want are not good for us, and therefore, God will not give them to us. He even protects us from ourselves.

When God does a miracle to provide for your needs, make a decision to tell another person about it. This will encourage others to trust Him more!

Live the Life

For this lesson segment, choose one of the following activities, then do it to apply God's word to your life:

1. In your Bible look up Matthew 6:25-34. Write or type out the verses on a piece of paper or index cards. Then, over the course of this study, memorize them to help you when you begin to worry about your provision.

2. Whenever you start to worry about your provision or other circumstances in your life, play a Christian CD or DVD, or sing some Christian praise and worship music. When you begin to sing, it will encourage your heart and help you get your focus back on God. Our adversary, Satan, likes to bombard us with thoughts to try to get us depressed or doubting God. When the music or singing begins, he won't hang around, because he doesn't like it when we worship God!

3. Make a list of things you need God to provide for you. List items specifically. For example, if you need money for rent, list it as 'money for rent.' If you need food, medical care or clothing, list it as such. When your list is complete, keep it, and pray every day for your needs. Then wait and watch to see how God will provide!

4. If you have been blessed by God and do not have any needs at this time, consider giving something to someone else in need. If you don't know someone in need, check to see if you have a local food bank, mission, or some other organization that helps needy people in your area, and make a donation. Your donation can be food, clothing, money or other material goods, to help someone with their needs. By giving, you demonstrate God's love to others!

Review, Reflect, and Respond

As you review this week's lesson, make a list of the things you've learned on the journal page for this lesson. If possible, share some of these with other believers to encourage them to trust God more.

Close in Prayer

Thank God for His awesome provision for our lives! If you have needs, pray and ask God for those things. Also pray for any other people you know that have needs. Ask God to help us trust Him more!

Lesson 3

God Is Everywhere

"Where can I go from Your Spirit?
Or where can I flee from Your presence?
If I ascend into heaven, You are there,
if I make my bed in hell, behold, You are there.
If I take the wings of the morning, and
dwell in the uttermost parts of the sea,
even there Your hand shall lead me,
and Your right hand shall hold me."
--Psalm 139:7-10

Open in Prayer

Ask God to show you that He is there in your life. Then watch to see how God confirms His presence to you. Some ways in which God confirms His presence include: An unexpected provision, a Christian coming by to share God's word or fellowship, a sudden opportunity to help someone in need or share God's word, or a miracle God works out in your life's circumstances. These are only a few of the ways God moves among His people.

Memory Verses

Spend a few minutes each day meditating on the opening verses and memorizing them. Continue working until you have them firmly planted in your memory.

Beginning Activity

Can you remember a time when you wanted to run away from God and/ or His will in your life? Perhaps you were hurt? Or maybe God didn't answer a prayer the way you wanted Him to answer it? Or perhaps God didn't heal a loved one when you wanted Him to, or He allowed great trial and suffering in your life, and you became so discouraged that you wanted to give up on God? If you can remember a time like this, write about it on the journal page for this lesson. Then pray and ask God to help you trust Him more, even in difficult circumstances. Also remember God is everywhere, including being there with you. If you're God's child, He will never leave you or forsake you—even if you give up on Him.

Lesson Introduction

In this lesson we look at an attribute of God called 'omnipresence.' This is a large word meaning 'everywhere present.' Being everywhere present doesn't mean God lives in the molecules of lifeless, earthly creations such as rocks and other objects. God's Spirit is everywhere in the atmosphere of the heavens and the earth, and He is "everywhere present" at the same time. God exists outside of created things, yet He will inhabit the hearts of people who have been "born again," and have experienced "new birth" by the Holy Spirit.

John 4:24 tells us, "God is Spirit (...)." During new birth, our spirits are "quickened" or "made alive" through our repentance and acceptance of Jesus, and the work He accomplished when He died on the cross, was buried, and rose from the tomb on the third day. Through "new birth" by the Holy Spirit, we have been reconciled to God, through the blood of Jesus Christ. Now we can come boldly to the throne of God, and receive grace in the time of need, through prayer and relationship with God.

In Psalm 139:7-12 David wrote, "Where can I go from Your Spirit? Or where can I flee from Your Presence? If I ascend into heaven, You are there; If I make my bed in hell, behold, You are there. If I take the wings of the morning, and dwell in the uttermost parts of the sea, even there Your hand shall lead me, and Your right hand shall hold me. If I say, 'Surely the darkness shall fall on me,' even the night shall be light about me; indeed the darkness shall not hide from You, but the night shines as the day; the darkness and the light are both alike to You.'"

In this lesson we look at one of many places in Scripture where God's omnipresence is revealed. God can see everything at the same time because of His attribute of omnipresence. Proverbs 15:3 tells us, "The eyes of the Lord are in every place, keeping watch on the evil and the good."

"Behold, the Lord's hand is not shortened, that it cannot save; nor His ear heavy, that it cannot hear. But your iniquities have separated you from your God; and your sins have hidden His face from you, so that He will not hear." (Isaiah 59:1)

"The Redeemer will come to Zion, and to those who turn from transgression in Jacob," says the Lord." (Isaiah 59:20)

Perhaps this lesson will help you understand how impossible it is to get away from God. He loves us so much He keeps pursuing us, even when we don't want Him around. God alone understands our great need for Him, and thankfully, He won't give up on us easily. Even when we reject Him, God still continues loving us, and hoping we will change our minds, and come to Him. Even when we deny His presence (denying it won't take it away), God still reaches out with His eternal, everlasting and unfailing love! Wow! How different it would be if we loved one another as God loves us!

In the Word

Read the short book of Jonah this week. Though the reading is a little longer than most, it is necessary to get the whole story of Jonah, and his attempt to run away from God. The book of Jonah contains some great lessons for all of us!

Questions to Consider

1. What task did God ask Jonah to do in Nineveh?

2. What did Jonah do in response to God's request?

3. Did God manage to find Jonah?

4. How did God convince Jonah to do the work He asked of him?

5. What lesson did God try to teach Jonah by using the plant He gave Jonah for shade?

Journal Activity

Choose one of the following activities and write a paragraph about it on your journal page for this lesson:

1. How do you think you would feel if the sailors on your ship threw you overboard to calm a storm? What would you do if you were Jonah, and the sailors cast lots, and the lot fell to you? Can you think of any solutions to the problem other than having the sailors throw you into the sea?

2. Can you think of a time when you tried to run away from God and found yourself in a bad predicament because of it? How did you finally resolve this situation?

3. How do you think you would feel if you were in the belly of a big fish for three days and three nights? Can you imagine what it looked like inside of the fish? Can you imagine how cold and dark it must have been? What about the smell?

4. Do you think Jonah had the sailors throw him overboard because he had the faith to believe God would rescue him? Or do you think Jonah wanted to die to escape the task God had for him to do?

Decisions for Life:

The story of Jonah shows us God is everywhere. Because God is Spirit, He is omnipresent. God was with Jonah all the time and God knew what Jonah was trying to do. There is no way Jonah could have disappeared from God.

Like Jonah, God is also with His people, and there is no way we can hide from Him. God is always with us, in our hearts, no matter how far away we try to run! Thank God that because of His omnipresence, He always knows when we need His help, and He's always there to rescue us!

If you've been trying to hide or run away from God, know He is everywhere, and every time you run away from God, you run into God. He knows where you are, and what you are doing. If this is your circumstance, make a decision to repent, turn away from your sin, and do what God has required of you. Learn from Jonah by realizing that Jonah would have saved himself a lot of trouble if he had only done it God's way the first time.

Also, when Jonah didn't get his way, he got angry, and had a pity party. He tried to justify his anger, and get God to take his life. How often do we get angry because we don't get our way? How often do we have pity parties or temper tantrums, and try to justify them, even when we are wrong? If you struggle with this, pray and ask God to help you overcome this challenge.

If we have pity on animals and plants but have no pity for our fellow human beings, we have our priorities messed up. People are eternal, and God's Son, Jesus Christ, gave His life for them. They are precious in God's sight! Scripture tells us, "Those who trust in their wealth and boast in the multitude of their riches, none of them can by any means redeem his brother, nor give to God a ransom for him—for the redemption of their souls is costly, and it shall cease forever—that he should continue to live eternally, and not see the pit." (Psalm 49:6-9)

Jonah had pity on his withered plant, but he failed to see the value of the souls of the people in Nineveh. How many of us get our priorities messed up and fail to see the value of the souls of the people we encounter every day? If this is true in your life, make a decision to ask God to help you see the value of those around you through His eyes. Then pray and ask God to help you value people more.

Jonah knew God well enough to know He was difficult to get away from, so he ran far away, and tried to escape from God. But Jonah found out God knew everything, and God was right there with him all the time. Jonah could not escape the presence of God because God is everywhere.

If you need comfort or help with a challenge in your life, call out and ask God to intervene in your situation. God is there, and He will work on your behalf because He loves you. Behold, God is awesome because He's everywhere present!

Live the Life

Choose one of the following activities to complete in order to help you learn how to apply this lesson to your daily life:

1. If God has been asking you to do something for Him but you haven't obeyed, step out and do it, knowing He will be with you all the time. God will bless you for your obedience! Then write a paragraph about the experience in your journal.

2. If you know someone who is trying to run away from God and/ or something God wants them to do, pray for them every day for a week. If you feel God leading you to speak to them, encourage them, in a loving way, to do what God has asked of them. Perhaps you could even share the story of Jonah with them.

3. If you know someone who is discouraged and/or thinks God has forsaken them, encourage them, and let them know God is there. Let them know He is only a prayer away. Perhaps you can even pray with them because God is just waiting for them to cry out to Him! God will hear your prayer because God is there; He's everywhere!

4. When God speaks to you about working on an area of your life, write about it on the journal page for this lesson. Make a note

of what God is speaking to you, and make a choice to ask God to help you in this area so—together—you can overcome it. God will help you with His divine power!

Review, Reflect, and Respond

Spend some time reviewing this lesson. Then make a list of the things you've learned on your journal page. Save your list so you can periodically review it, and remember how awesome God is.

Close in Prayer

Thank God for His attribute of omnipresence. Ask Him to help you in your areas of struggle. God wants us to ask Him for the things we need, and He wants to help! God wants to be included in our daily lives. God wants us to have a personal, one-on-one relationship with Him through prayer, reading His Word, and fellowship with Him throughout our day. Ask God to help you get to know Him better, and to help you behold His awesome presence in the world around you. God wants to know you personally!

Lesson 4

God Is Big!

"Thus says the Lord:
'Heaven is My throne, and the earth is My footstool.
Where is the house that you will build Me?
And where is the place of My rest?'"
--Isaiah 66:1

"Do you not know that you are the temple of God
and that the Spirit of God dwells in you?
If anyone defiles the temple of God,
God will destroy him.
For the temple of God is holy, which temple you are."
--1 Corinthians 3:16-17

Open in Prayer

As you begin this lesson with prayer, ask God to reveal His awesome character to you, and to help you receive what He has for you. Also ask God to help you get a bigger perception of who He is, and to help you learn to trust Him more. In addition, ask God to help you understand that it's impossible for men or women to ever compare to Him in ability, knowledge, power, or anything else.

Memory Verses

Spend some time each day this week planting the memory verses in your heart and mind. Don't give up until you have them memorized. If you find any unfamiliar words in the verses, look them up in a dictionary, and write the meaning of each word in the margin on this page. You can refer to the definitions later as you study this lesson.

Beginning Activity: Too Big!

Think about what happens when you try putting an extremely large quantity of liquid from one container into an extremely small container, or do the reverse. This was an object lesson I used in children's classes and it's really simple, so we won't actually do it. Yet, we can gain some great insights through thinking about what would happen if we really did it.

Imagine yourself standing at a counter space, near a sink. You have one extra-large container (at least one gallon) filled with water. You also have the smallest sized container you could find, such as a small plastic bottle or even a small measuring spoon. Next, you try to pour water from the large container into the small one, allowing it to overflow just enough to see what happens. As you visualize this scene, ask yourself the following questions:

1. What happens when you try to put too much of something into a container that's too small?

2. Is it possible for all of the water from the big container to fit in the little one?

3. Is it possible for the water in the little container to equal or fill the big one?

4. How can God be like the big container, and we be like the small one?

Write the answers to the above questions on the journal page for this lesson. Then read the rest of the following information.

As finite people we sometimes try to put a large, divine God into a small container, such as a man-made temple, man-made plans, or a mental box, we have perceived about God in our minds. But our minds, and our perceptions of God, are not nearly large enough to hold or understand all of Him. Some people believe they have God figured out, and have complete perceptions of Him in their minds. Other people would rather keep their small perception of God than choose to read His word, find out the truth, and get a bigger perception of Him. But God is not limited or contained within a person's perception or mental picture of who He is.

Also, as humans, we sometimes try to fit God into our ideals, beliefs, and our human thinking. But the complete presence of God cannot fit into our limited thinking because He is too big, and His ways are not our ways. God knows and understands so much more than we do. We cannot even fathom His simple statements such as "I love you with an everlasting love." No matter how hard we try, we will never be able to fully understand God and His ways, because our finite minds are simply too small to contain the knowledge of the fullness of God.

The water in the large container is a small, but illustrative example of God's presence. God pours His presence into our lives, but we can only contain and understand a small portion of Him. All the water that overflows into the bowl is representative of God's presence coming from our hearts, and flowing into the lives of those around us. We cannot contain God. But by refusing to believe or obey parts of Scripture that we don't like, we can harden our own hearts. Our hardened hearts are stopped up, and God will not use a vessel that has sin in his or her heart, until repentance comes forth. If we have sin in our hearts, the flow of the Holy Spirit that God desires to pour into our hearts, does not flow through us, or into the lives of others.

Sometimes we try to make God fit into our lives and plans, instead of trying to fit into His. People cannot fit God's divine being or plans into their limited perceptions, because God is too big! Like the small container, we try to hold and understand as much about God as possible, and this is good. However, sometimes we get puffed up with our knowledge, and because we think we know so much, we forget we are only a small container. We also forget that no matter how hard we try, we can never be a big container.

We must come to understand we are like the small container, and God is bigger than our greatest imaginations or knowledge bases. God's wisdom and understanding are infinitely bigger than ours. If we think we can ever compare with God, contain Him, stop Him from accomplishing His plans, or become like God, we are deceived! It is simply impossible.

As we move forward in this lesson, I challenge you to tear apart the box or perception you have of God, and to get into His word to learn more about who He truly is. Let's not try to put God in our limited boxes, or our perceptions of "how we want Him to be." Rather, let's consider and believe who God's word tells us He is, and leave the door open for our perception to change and grow, as we learn more about God from His word, and our personal relationship with Him.

Lesson Introduction

In this lesson we look at God's intervention in the lives of two of His servants, King David, and King Solomon. We will get a glimpse of how vast God is, how much He loved King David, and how God demonstrated His divine power and love in the lives of both kings.

God made David and Solomon many wonderful promises, and fulfilled them. The fulfillment of these promises shows one example of God's ability to know the future, and bring forth His plans, even if His plan seems impossible.

King David, the father of King Solomon, planned to build a temple for God. God revealed His plans for the great temple to David, who held on to them, and later passed them on to King Solomon. Though David wanted to build the temple, God would not allow him to build it. But God promised David that his son, Solomon, would become the heir to his kingdom, and the builder of the temple.

When Solomon grew up and became king, he took the plans God had given David and built an awesome temple for God. The temple had much gold overlay, and fine craftsmanship. For a time, the glory of God filled that temple.

But God is so big that His complete presence is too big to live in any temple made by human hands. As we see in our memory verses, Heaven is God's throne, and the Earth is His footstool.

Now, as a result of Jesus' death and resurrection, God has a new temple in which His Spirit dwells. God is so big He fills the heavens and the earth with His presence, and His being is everywhere. Even though God is so big, by the Holy Spirit, He made His new dwelling place in the hearts of men and women who are "born again" by the work of the Holy Spirit. In 1 Corinthians 6:19-20 scripture tells us, "Or do you not know that your body is the temple of the Holy Spirit, who is in you, whom you have from God, and you are not your own? For you were bought at a price; therefore, glorify God in your body and in your spirit, which are God's."

Being "born again" means we have asked God to forgive us of our sins, and invited Him to come and live in our hearts, and be our Lord and

Savior. When we are born again, God quickens our spirit and makes it alive, and gives us a new heart and the mind of Christ. Then we begin losing our desires for the ungodly things the world promotes, and gaining new desires for the things of God. As we continue our relationship with God, we grow spiritually, and desire to live godly lives to please Him. We make a U-turn in our life, and the people around us can see the Holy Spirit at work in us!

God wants us to know He loves us, and He is BIG and able enough to take care of us. So let's dig into His Word and learn more about our awesome God!

In the Word

Before you read this week's lesson you should know the Bible Story has been paraphrased, and shortened, to help you get more information with far less reading. For those who want to do the research and read the scriptures for themselves, the following list of passages will provide you with much of the information from the story: 1 Kings, chapters 3, 6 and 10, 1 Kings 8:1-30, 9:1-3; Ephesians 3:16-17 and 2 Corinthians 6:16. I encourage you to dig in and read the scriptures for yourself!

King David, King Solomon, and the Temple of God

King David, as a young boy, was chosen by God to be anointed, and declared the future king of Israel. As a shepherd boy for his father's family, David was anointed by God's prophet, Samuel. At this time a man named Saul was king. David grew up under Saul's authority and eventually became a soldier in Saul's army. Saul eventually disobeyed God, and turned away from Him. God's Spirit left Saul, and Saul and his sons eventually lost their lives in a military battle.

After Saul's death, David became king over Israel. God referred to David as the "Apple of His eye." David loved God, and walked with Him. Though David made many mistakes—some extremely serious—he repented, and kept walking with God. God loved David and blessed his life.

Because David loved God, he desired to build God a magnificent temple, a place in which to rest the Ark of the Covenant of the Lord and to be a dwelling place for God. However, God had different plans. God would not allow David to build the great temple because David had shed too much human blood. But God told David his son, Solomon, would oversee the building of the great temple. This was one of many wonderful promises God made to David. God also promised David his seed would rule over David's kingdom forever. God is at work fulfilling His promise, and someday, Jesus Christ, the Messiah, will return and take His proper place as King of the Jews. He will rule and reign on this earth through the Millennium (for 1,000 years) and then throughout eternity!

God revealed His plans for the temple to David who recorded every detail. These plans were kept safe until God's plan unfolded, and Solomon would rule over the kingdom of Israel, and build the temple for God. Before his death, King David made his son, Solomon, king and gave him plans for the temple, surrounding areas, treasuries, and all the articles to be used in the temple. David even had instructions for those serving in the temple, and for the chariot, that is, "…the cherubim of gold that spread their wings, sheltering the Ark of the Covenant of God," known as the "Mercy seat." "All this," said David, "The LORD made me understand in writing, by His hand upon me, all the works of these plans." (1 Chronicles 28:18-19)

David told his son, Solomon, to be strong and courageous, and do the work. He also told Solomon not to be afraid or discouraged because the Lord God was with him, and wouldn't fail or forsake him, and the Priests, Levites, and willing people would obey his commands.

It was a bittersweet moment for Solomon, one of great pain amidst the overwhelming joy of becoming the new king of Israel, and heir to his father, King David's, throne. Only a short time had passed since his father had passed away from illness, and Solomon clearly remembered the moment when his dying father passed the throne on to him. Governing this nation would be an enormous, but joyous task. This moment, however, was anything but joyous. Solomon was in agony because the task immediately set before him was ordering his men to put his own brother, Adonija, to death for attempting to take over the throne of Israel. Adonija was caught conspiring against him, and Solomon knew that Israel would not have peace as long as Adonija lived.

After Solomon gave the command and secured his throne, the Lord appeared to him in a dream and said, "Ask for whatever you want me to give you."

Solomon asked God to give him a discerning heart to govern the people, and to distinguish between right and wrong. The Lord granted Solomon's wish, giving him a wise and discerning heart, with so much wisdom that Solomon's wisdom far exceeded any other people during his lifetime. The Lord promised Solomon that if he walked in the ways of the Lord, and obeyed His statutes and commands, he would be given a long life. God fulfilled His promises to Solomon.

Solomon and the workers completed the temple in seven years, and it was covered with gold, in much of it. Then Solomon had all the furnishings and dedicated things brought to the temple. Then the priests brought the Ark of the Covenant to its place in the inner sanctuary of the temple, called "the Most Holy Place." Finally, the priests withdrew from the Holy Place, and joined the Levites in praising the Lord in unison.

The temple of the Lord was filled with a cloud. The priests could not perform their service because of the cloud, for the glory of the Lord filled the temple.

Though the glory of the Lord filled that temple, God's presence is everywhere. Because God is a spirit being, He can—like clouds or smoke—fill any size container He desires to fill. Yet, because of the omnipresence of God, no "container" can hold all of His presence—not even a huge temple.

Solomon, in a prayer before the whole assembly of Israel, put it this way: "But will God indeed dwell with men on the earth? Behold, heaven and the heaven of heavens cannot contain You. How much less this temple which I have built!" (2 Chronicles 6:18)

Isaiah 66:1 says, "Thus says the LORD: 'Heaven is My throne, And earth is My footstool. Where is the house that you will build Me? And where is the place of My rest?'"

Later in life, Solomon married and loved many women from foreign places. As Solomon grew older, his wives turned his heart after other foreign gods, which led him astray. Solomon's heart was not fully devoted to the Lord God, as the heart of his father, David, had been.

Now God's earthly dwelling place is within the hearts of men and women who believe and receive the work Jesus did on the cross at Calvary, and who are "born again" by God's Holy Spirit. Scripture tells us, "For it is the God who commanded light to shine out of darkness, who has shone in our hearts to give the light of the knowledge of the glory of God in the face of Jesus Christ." (2 Corinthians 4:6) Ecclesiastes 3:11 tells us, "He has made everything beautiful in its time. Also He has put eternity in their hearts, except that no one can find out the work that God does from beginning to end."

Behold our awesome God! He blesses and makes wonderful promises to men and women—and He keeps His promises! God has fulfilled the beautiful promises He made to King David, and King Solomon.

31

God continued loving them, even though they did many things that did not please Him.

God also loves us, even when we fall and sin against Him. When we fall into sin, God's wonderful love immediately causes Him to go into the action of restoring us to Himself by convicting us of our sin, which we should confess, ask forgiveness for, and go forward, trying our best not to repeat that sin again. Yet even if we fail, God will never stop loving us!

Questions to Consider

1. What great dream did David have in regards to God's presence?

2. Why was David not allowed to build this dream?

3. Who did God put in David's place as king after David died?

4. In addition to ruling over Israel, what big task did Solomon accomplish?

5. After the task was complete, what did Solomon realize?

Journal Activity

In your journal for this lesson write a paragraph about one of the following:

1. Do you have a dream about something great you would like to do for God? If so, write a paragraph explaining what your dream is; then pray and ask God if this is what He wants you to do. Respond accordingly.

2.   If you could ask God for any desire you might have, what would it be? Write a list of your desires—and your reasons for wanting them—in your journal. Then pray, believing God will answer your prayer for these desires of your heart.

3.   During this week search your heart and mind to see if your perception of God makes Him smaller or larger than the Bible tells us He is? Do you believe God is bigger than the heavens can contain? Or do you look at God as little more than a man? Write an entry in your journal describing about how big you perceive God to be?

4.   Do you think any person can ever compare with God's greatness and size? Why or why not? Write a short essay comparing God's greatness to ours. Conclude your essay with your final decision regarding the greatness of God as compared to that of people.

Decisions for Life

In our lesson this week we learned God is big! You were also encouraged to look at your perception of God, and compare it to what the Bible tells us about Him. Make a decision to read the Bible every day, and learn more about God, and His ways. Reading God's word is the only way we can get a correct perspective on spiritual things. While we are reading, the Holy Spirit will bring revelation, and lead and guide us into the truth. When we compare our perceptions to God's truths, we can find out about our wrong perceptions, and ask God to help us correct them.

Also make a decision to believe God is big, and He is able to take care of you. Ask God to help you trust Him more. God's primary work is for people to believe and be saved. God gave His One and only Son so we could be saved, and become the children of God. Behold our awesome God!

Live the Life

Complete one of the following activities to apply this week's lesson to your life:

1. Pray and ask God for a miracle in your life, or in the life of someone you know. Pray for that miracle every day for a week. Believe, and know God is big, and He is able to do that miracle for you!

2. Do you have a task God has asked you to do? Pray for God's direction and guidance; then step out and begin the work God has given you. In your journal, write a paragraph about what you believe God has for you to do, and about any experiences you may have had (such as visions, words from the Lord, etc.) that confirm God wants you to do this task for Him. Refer back to your writing periodically to refresh your memory about God's call on your life. This will encourage you to press on toward the finish line!

3. Do you have a desire stirring in your heart about a way of serving God or His people in your local community? If so, pray and ask God for His leading; ask Him to open the doors He wants you to go through, and to close the doors He doesn't want you to go through. Then step out in boldness, and go get involved! God will close the door on things He doesn't want you doing, but He desires that we serve Him, and others. As we move, He directs. Write about your experience on your journal page for this lesson.

4. If you know someone who is going through difficult tests and trials, share this week's Bible story with them. Then encourage them that God is big enough to take care of them as well. Pray God will divinely intervene in their circumstances.

Review, Reflect, and Respond

Take some time to review this lesson and reflect on what you've learned. Then write a paragraph on your journal page, detailing what you've gained from this lesson.

Close in Prayer

Pray for the people in your circle of influence, including yourself. Ask God to help everyone get a bigger perception of Him. Also ask God to reveal Himself to those you prayed for, and help them to trust Him more. As the darkness continues to spread throughout our world, people will need to come to the place where they can trust God to take care of every one of their needs.

Lesson 5

God Is a Personal God

"O Lord, You have searched me and known me.
You know my sitting down and my rising up;
You understand my thought afar off.
You comprehend my path and my lying down,
and are acquainted with all my ways.
For there is not a word on my tongue, but behold,
O Lord, You know it altogether.
You have hedged me behind and before,
and laid Your hand upon me."
--Psalm 139:1-5

"For You formed my inward parts;
You covered me in my mother's womb.
I will praise You, for I am fearfully and wonderfully made;
marvelous are Your works, and that my soul knows very well."
--Psalm 139:13-14

Open in Prayer

Many people, living in various countries across the globe, believe in all kinds of different gods. Yet these gods are not real or personal gods. Yahweh is the only true God, and He meets people on a personal level. Yahweh knows each one of us completely, yet still loves us with an unfailing, everlasting love. Yahweh accepts us as we are, and loves us more than any human being ever can. So in your prayer, ask God (Yahweh) to show you how personal He is, to reveal Himself to you and show you how much He cares, even about the small details of your life.

Next, ask God to show you any sin in your life which you have not repented from. Ask God to forgive you, cleanse you, and help you overcome in that area of your life. God is a God who convicts us of personal sin so we can repent, be cleansed, and have an intimate relationship with Him. He does this with a heart of love—not to be mean or to withhold good things from us—but to restore us into right relationship with Him. Also ask God to help us see the love in His act of confronting sin in our hearts. God doesn't want to condemn us; He doesn't want us to perish in our sin. God wants us to overcome and become members in His heavenly household!

Memory Verses

Take a few minutes each day this week to memorize the opening verses. Complete the memorization by the end of the week. Notice God knows all of our thoughts. He knows when we have sin in our heart, and He's just waiting for us to come Him, repent and be cleansed and restored, because He wants us to have a personal relationship with Him. God loves us so!

Beginning Activity

Take some time to read through Psalm 139 and write down the lines that speak of how well God knows each one of us. Then write a paragraph stating how you feel knowing your God knows you so intimately. Do you sense His love? Do you feel exposed? How do you feel about God knowing every one of your personal thoughts? From reading God's word, wouldn't you agree God is a personal God?

Lesson Introduction

Millions of people are bound up by the enemy of their souls because of false religious systems that teach about impersonal gods who are just waiting for someone to make a mistake so He can punish them. These gods are false gods; they can never compare to Yahweh, the God of Abraham, Isaac, and Jacob.

Yahweh, the God of Israel, is a loving, personal Father who knows every detail about us and still loves us deeply—more than any human ever could. Psalm 139 gives us a great picture of how Yahweh is personal with each one of us. Yahweh loves men, women, and children, even when they make mistakes—even big ones! Though, at times, Yahweh disciplines those He loves, He doesn't do it just to be mean. He does it to correct, train, and make us overcomers. He does not lie in wait for us to make mistakes just so He can punish us.

Yahweh's nature is love, in fact **He IS** love, and He demonstrated His love by sending His Only begotten Son, Jesus, to save us. John 3:16-17 says, "For God so loved the world that He gave His only begotten Son, that whoever believes in Him should not perish but have everlasting life. For God did not send His Son into the world to condemn the world, but that the world through Him might be saved."

God loves us so much He sent His one and only Son to pay the penalty we deserve because of our sin. God's Son came to destroy the works of the devil and the power of sin over our lives. He also came to make a way for each one of us to become adopted children in God's heavenly household. Now that's a personal God! You can't get much more personal than becoming a member of God's family!

In this lesson we look at a situation where God gets personal and confronts one of His children, a man and king, about his personal sin. God sends His prophet, Nathan, to the king to confront him, and give him a chance to repent, be forgiven, and be restored. God loved this man enough to confront him, in love, and save him from eternal death and destruction.

God loves each one of us, and He will confront us with knowledge of our personal sin. As God convicts us of sin, He wants us to confess it to Him, ask for forgiveness, and turn away from the sin. God does this because He knows personal sin can kill us, and it can keep us from entering into His kingdom. God wants to make sure sin is dealt with so we can be forgiven, cleansed, and reconciled to Him. So let's look at this week's scripture passage.

In the Word

Read 2 Samuel 11:1-12:27. Then proceed to the 'Questions to Consider' segment.

Questions to Consider

1. What did King David do after he saw the beautiful woman bathing from the roof of his palace?

2. What did David's desire tempt him to finally do to the woman's husband?

3. What message did God's prophet, Nathan, have to deliver to the king?

4. What verdict did King David pronounce on the man in Nathan's story?

5. How did King David respond when he found out Nathan was speaking about him?

Journal Activity

On the journal page for this lesson, write a response to one of the following items below:

1. Have you ever desired to have something so much you deceived others and sinned against God to get it?

2. Can you remember a time when the Lord used another person to confront you about your personal sin?

3. Can you remember a time when you were deeply affected by the great forgiveness and mercy of God?

4. How does it make you feel knowing God is personal, and He loves you, and wants you to become a member of His kingdom and His heavenly household?

Decisions for Life

During this study we've looked at true stories from scripture that show us how God meets His people on a personal level. We've seen that God provides, heals, convicts, forgives, and restores His people according to their personal needs.

As we've studied this week, have you thought of a personal need you would like God to provide? Do you need a healing? Or do you sense the Holy Spirit convicting you of a sin which has not yet been dealt with? If so, write down your need or confession in the space below:

Today I want to encourage you to make a decision to ask God for forgiveness from your sin, or to provide for any need you may have. Write out a prayer to your God about your decision in the space below:

Live the Life

Complete one of the following activities in order to put what you've learned from this lesson into practice:

1. On your journal page, make a list of people you know who have need of God's provision in their lives. Beside each name, list a specific need they have. Pray every day this week for God to answer the list of needs. Share any praise reports with someone who needs to be encouraged.

2. On your journal page for this lesson, make a list of people who need God's healing touch. List the specific needs by each person's name. Then pray every day for a week that God will heal the people on your list. Share any praise reports with someone who needs reassurance that God is still in the healing business.

3. Make a list of areas in your personal life where you need God's help in overcoming personal sin. Pray for God's forgiveness, and then ask God to help you in these areas. Then turn away from the sin, and go forward, trying not to fall back into it again.

4. In your journal, write a short story about a time when God intervened in your life in a special way. Share your story with

someone who needs to know God is a personal God who knows their needs, and cares about them very much.

5. Read Psalm 51, in which David wrote about his experience with sin, and when Nathan the prophet came and confronted him. On your journal page, write down the lines of scripture where David pleads with God to forgive him for his sin.

Review, Reflect, and Respond

Spend some time reviewing this lesson. Then write down some things you've learned this week. Then write a paragraph responding to the following question: Do you think people would learn as much from their mistakes if God took away all of the consequences of personal sin? Why or why not?

Close in Prayer

If God has convicted you of personal sin, please deal with it by praying, asking God for forgiveness, and turning away from the sin. If you have sinned against another person, you may need to go and apologize to that person, and then make things right between you and God. When you pray, confess your sin to God. He wants to forgive you. God is a personal God who loves you unconditionally, and wants to spend time with you every day.

If you know some people with personal needs, take time to pray for them. Pray for any needs you may have as well. God wants to show you how much He loves you, and He wants you to love Him too! Behold! Our God is a personal God!

Lesson 6

God Is Love

"Beloved, let us love one another, for love is of God,
and everyone who loves is born of God and knows God.
He who does not love does not know God, for God is love.
In this the love of God was manifested toward us,
that God has sent His Only Begotten Son into the world,
that we might live through Him.
In this is love, not that we loved God, but that He loved us
and sent His Son to be the propitiation for our sins."
--1 John 4:7-10

Open in Prayer

Ask God to reveal the truth of His unconditional love to you. Ask Him to show you how much He loves you, and how much He cares about even the small details of your life.

As a Christian believer, there have been many times that I've lost my keys or misplaced important papers. At other times I had needs for food or other small items. Nearly every time I prayed, God came through for me, and I know He can do the same for you! He wants us to come to Him with our needs, whether they are large or small. God wants to take care of us because He loves us!

Memory Verses

Take a few minutes each day of this week and work toward planting the memory verses in your heart and mind. Complete the memorization by the end of the week. As you work on the verses, meditate on the words you say. Let the word of God work in your heart and mind. God gave His Son as a sacrifice for us, we should be able to spend at least a few minutes of our day with Him!

Beginning Activity

Consider what you already know about love. Take a few minutes to think about it; then, write out your definition of love on the journal page for this lesson.

After completing this lesson, reread your definition of love, and make any changes that you need to make. Have you added or changed anything about it? If so, why did you change it? Write down any new conclusions about love on your journal page.

Lesson Introduction

In this lesson we look at God's nature, which is love. We will see how God demonstrates His love toward us. We will also look at Paul's great description of God's true, pure agape love.

As human beings, we cannot comprehend the great, unconditional love God has for each one of us; nor can we love like God does, in our own human effort. But God can work through us to love others with the love He pours into our hearts and lives. John 3:16-18 tells us, "For God so loved the world that He gave His only begotten Son, that whoever believes in Him should not perish but have everlasting life. For God did not send His Son into the world to condemn the world, but that the world through Him might be saved. He who believes in Him is not condemned, but He who does not believe is condemned already, because He has not believed in the name of the only begotten Son of God."

Many people in the world, both Christians and unbelievers, do not understand the true definition of love. We think of love as a warm, fuzzy feeling we get when we meet a special person who we want to share our lives with. However, love is not only a warm feeling—it is a commitment. Love is not seeking a partner only to fulfill our own selfish desires. It is not seeking a partner so we can get what we want from them, and then toss them and their feelings aside, or divorce them, so we can move on to the next person who happens to come our way. **No!** True love is commitment, and putting your own desires aside, when necessary, for the benefit of the one you love. Love says, "How may I meet a need in your life?" As we step out and try to meet the needs of our loved one, our needs, in turn, will also be met!

God gave us an awesome demonstration of love when He sacrificed His precious Son, Jesus Christ, so we could be saved from sin and eternal death, and become adopted members in God's family. God loves Jesus, and didn't want to see Him die on a cruel cross, and suffer so much, when Jesus was without sin. Yet God knew this was the only way He could save us. God needed a pure sacrifice to pay the penalty for our sin, and we could never be pure without His intervention. So Jesus yielded to the Father's will and plan, and died on the cross so He could save us from our sin! Then, after three days in the tomb, God raised Jesus from the dead, and eventually up to heaven to sit at the right hand of God. As Jesus sits by the Father, He continually prays, interceding on our behalf. Because God loved us so much, He went ahead with His plan, sacrificing His Son for us.

Jesus prayed several times that the cup be taken from Him. But since it was the Father's will, He willingly obeyed and suffered on our behalf. Here we see Jesus' humanity, as well as His yielding to the Father's will, for us. Jesus could have called for 10,000 angels to come and rescue Him. Yet, because He also loved us and could see the joy that was set before Him beyond the cross, He chose to obey the Father's will, and die for us. God, all three persons—Father, Son and the Holy Spirit—are awesome examples of God's love for us. All three work together to express this agape love which lays down its life for another person. That's commitment, and our awesome God did this when we were His enemies! Our God is our supreme example of love!

In marriage, husbands and wives should submit to one another in love, and put their partner's well being above their own. For more description and details about God's kind of love, read 1 Corinthians, chapter 13. You will see a description of this love which truly means "giving" of one's self for another's happiness. If both, the husband and wife, would think this way, there would not be as many divorces and broken families. Love is not easy, but it is the greatest gift any person can get or give. In speaking of spiritual gifts, the Apostle Paul said, "And now abide faith, hope, love, these three; but the greatest of these is love." (1 Corinthians 13:13)

In this lesson we look at an overview of God's demonstration of love. We will see how God worked out His plan of redemption for mankind. So let's move on to learn more about God's wonderful gift of love.

In the Word

This week has a little more reading than normal, but it is necessary to show God's whole plan of redemption. Read the following passages: John 1:1-18; Luke 1:26-38; Luke 2:1-7; John 17:1-5; John 18:28-20:18; Mark 16:19-20; Romans 5:1-21. After you complete the reading, move ahead and answer the questions below.

Questions to Consider

1. In John 1:1-17, who does the text say is "the Word in flesh that dwelt among us?"

2. According to Matthew 1:18-25 and Luke 1:35 who is the Father of Mary's child? What was the child's name?

3. According to John 3:16-18 what work did God send Jesus to do?

4. What did the women find out had happened to Jesus when they went to His tomb?

5. According to Romans 5:6-8 what was demonstrated by the death of Christ?

Journal Activity

Read 1 Corinthians, chapter 13, and list the characteristics of God's love on your journal page. If there are any words you don't understand, look up the definitions in a dictionary, and write them down in your journal as well. Note any new things you've learned about love.

Decisions for Life

In this week's lesson we read that the Word was with God in the beginning, and the Word was God. Then we read "the Word became flesh and dwelt among us," but the world did not recognize Him. John 1:14 says, "And the Word became flesh and dwelt among us, and we beheld His glory, the glory as of the only begotten of the Father, full of grace and truth." John 1:17 tells us the name of the one who came, who was 'full of grace and truth' saying, "(...) but grace and truth came through Jesus Christ."

Romans 5:5-10 says, "Now hope does not disappoint, because the love of God has been poured out in our hearts by the Holy Spirit who was given to us. For when we were still without strength, in due time Christ died for the ungodly. For scarcely for a righteous man will one die; yet perhaps for a good man someone would even dare to die. But God demonstrates His own love toward us, in that while we were still sinners, Christ died for us. Much more then, having now been justified by His blood, we shall be saved from wrath through Him. For if when we were enemies we were reconciled to God through the death of His Son, much more, having been reconciled, we shall be saved by His life."

In this week's lesson we've learned that God sent Jesus to earth to die and atone for our sins. God loved Jesus more than we can fathom, but He knew mankind could not provide the pure sacrifice needed to pay the penalty for our sins. Therefore God had to send Jesus. Jesus' sacrifice paid the penalty for mankind once and for all. There is no more need for a sacrificial lamb because the work is complete. Now we show our gratefulness and love for Jesus by obeying God's commands, loving God above all, and loving others—even our enemies. Once we accept the work Jesus did, and receive God's salvation, we are born again, and become adopted children of God, to whom He has given a great eternal inheritance. He has given us eternal life, treasures in heaven, adoption as sons, a place in His heavenly household, and forgiveness for our sins. That is truly a demonstration of love!

In this world many people have a selfish and/or warped understanding of true love. They think it is something they should get for themselves, instead of giving their lives for those they say they love. Others think intimate physical relationship is love, but that, by itself, is empty and is not love. Consider the attributes of love which we read about in 1

Corinthians, chapter 13. Not one of them speak of love being selfish or self-oriented.

This week I challenge you to make a decision to show more of the true, sacrificial love (as in 1 Corinthians 13) to those around you by doing special things for them. Giving others love instead of expecting love for yourself fulfills a need in you as well. When you only live for yourself, you do not get your need met. God fulfills your need when you love others unselfishly. Make a decision to become an example of Godly love, and commitment, to those around you, and help them learn the true meaning of 'love.' God is love, and He pours His love into the hearts and lives of His children, so we can pour it out to others!

Live the Life

Complete one of the following activities so you can put some of the points you've learned about love into practice in your daily life:

1. Take some time to come up with a definition for "sin." Write it down on the journal page for this lesson. Then take a brief time to meditate on your life, and consider if you have any unconfessed and/or unforgiven sin in your heart. Also examine the ways you have applied love to those other people in your life. Was it love or was it self-seeking? If you find any sin, write a prayer on your journal page, asking God to forgive you, and try not to repeat the sin. With His life and love, Jesus paid the price so you could be forgiven, cleansed by His blood, and covered with His righteousness!

2. Take some time to review the definition of love you wrote in the Beginning Activity. Compare your definition to the description of love in 1 Corinthians 13. Do you need to change your previous definition? If so, take time to rewrite the definition.

Then consider the definition of love, and ask yourself, "Do I demonstrate the true kind of love to those around me?" Then take some time to list ways you can express this love to those in your family. Then make love an action verb by doing some of the things on your list. Love without action is dead!

3. Read through the small book of 1 John, located toward the back of your Bible. As you read, take notes (on your journal page) of anything else you learn about love. Write a short response about what you've learned on the journal page for this lesson.

4. In your journal make a list of people who are close and special, to you. You can include family, friends, coworkers or anyone else who is a regular part of your daily life. Then, next to the person's name, list one thing you could do to appropriately demonstrate God's love to them. Then, during this week, try to do as many of these things for others as possible. After this week passes, continue demonstrating love to those around you.

5. Share the true meaning of love with those around you to help them understand that love's main goal is giving for the betterment of others—not seeking for self. Then, on your journal page, write down the responses of those you shared with. By doing this you may be able to help others in your family or circle of friends understand the true, Godly kind of love. Perhaps you can help them (especially teens and young adults) identify true love so they don't get mixed up in bad, self-seeking relationships. These kinds of relationships end up in the destruction of one or both people involved, and possibly others as well. People have enough confusion in life without repeatedly getting involved in bad relationships. The hurt from bad relationships may last throughout the person's lifetime. Only God can heal the deep-seated wounds from bad relationships! Thankfully, God can take these wounds, heal

them, and bring something good out of the destruction Satan intended to use to rob, destroy, or kill us. Behold, our God is awesome!

Review, Reflect, and Respond

Review the scripture passages you read in the segment called "In the Word." As you review, make an outline of the things you learned about the life of Jesus. When you're done, you should have a complete outline of God's plan of redemption of mankind. You can use this outline to review or share the Gospel with others.

Close in Prayer

Thank God for His wonderful demonstration of love in His sending Jesus to die, pay the penalty for our sin, and to make a way for us to become His adopted children, and members of His heavenly household. It's hard to comprehend the wonder of a God who would give up His only Son to atone for the sins of His enemies.

Also, ask God to help you understand His love, and to love others as He has loved you. Thank Him for giving us the demonstration of His love, and for pouring His love into our hearts so we can pour it out to those around us. What an awesome example of love God has given us. Behold, our awesome God is love!

Lesson 7

God Is Three-In-One

"Hear, O Israel: The Lord our God, the Lord is One."
--Deuteronomy 6:4

"For there are three that bear witness in heaven:
the Father, the Word, and the Holy Spirit;
and these three are one."
--1 John 5:7

"In the beginning was the Word,
and the Word was with God,
and the Word was God."
--John 1:1

"And the Word became flesh and dwelt among us,
and we beheld His glory;
the glory as of the only begotten of the Father,
full of grace and truth."
--John 1:14

Open in Prayer

Thank God for allowing us to learn about Him. Ask Him to open your heart and mind to receive what He has for you in this lesson. Pray God will reveal Himself to us, help us understand the meaning of 'three-in-one,' and show us some ways the three persons of God work together.

Memory Verses

Spend some time every day this week working towards the memorization of the opening verses. Challenge yourself to have them firmly planted in your heart and mind by the end of the week. Use them to teach or witness to others who want to know about our awesome God.

Beginning Activity

Consider an egg, which is commonly used in Sunday School classes to help explain the concept of "three-in-one" to children. According to "The Amazing Egg" by Susan James[1] (2002), the egg has five main parts: the yoke, the white, the membrane, the germ, and the outer shell."(p. 10) Together these parts make up one egg. However, since the membrane and germ are not readily seen, we use the three remaining parts—the yoke, white and shell—to illustrate the phrase "three-in-one." All three parts are needed to fulfill the purpose of bringing forth a newborn chick.

Each part of the egg has a special purpose in the creation of the baby chick. The hard white outer shell holds, and protects, the inner parts of the egg from sickness and disease. According to *The Amazing Egg* (James, 2002), the egg white and yoke provide nourishment for the growing baby animal." (p. 22) Without all of the parts of the egg, the embryo for the baby will not develop into a living being.

Take a few minutes and consider God. Do you know what role each person of the Godhead plays in creation? Do you know how they intercede in our lives? If you have an idea about this, write it down on the journal page for this lesson. Also, if you have any questions about the three-in-one God, write them down too. Then move ahead to the Lesson Introduction.

Lesson Introduction

Throughout Scripture we are told that God is a three-in-one being; three persons make up the Godhead. The three persons are God the Father, God the Son, and God the Holy Spirit. Together the three persons form one God. Other terms used to describe this attribute of God are "triune" or "trinity." We see this attribute of God revealed in Scripture throughout the Bible.

The oneness of God is a great mystery. Theology giants will continue to debate over the exact meaning of 'three-in-one' until Jesus returns, and reveals it to us. One view is the three persons of the Godhead are so intertwined that they cannot be separated. Another view is the "Oneness" means being in agreement, always. This is a true statement about the character of God, but Scripture doesn't give us a clear understanding of what "three-in-one" refers to, exactly. This great mystery is only one of many in the pages of the Bible. We will not understand it until we meet God face to face.

Scripture reveals that the three persons of God work together toward a single purpose. We see this "oneness" in the creation story, Jesus' baptism, and other places in Scripture. At Jesus' baptism, we see this unity in mind and purpose, as the three persons of God appear to confirm that Jesus is God's Son.

In this lesson we briefly explore the creation account and Jesus' baptism. In these accounts, the three persons of the Godhead appear, and work together, in agreement. The memory verses above also confirm this statement.

As we explore Scripture, I pray you will uncover nuggets of truth about God which you did not know before. On the day Jesus returns for His people, perhaps He will reveal the whole meaning, and whole truth, of this great mystery to us. Until then, we can explore Scripture, extract truth, and learn more about our awesome God.

Though Scripture tells us no one, except for Moses (Exodus 33:11), has ever seen God, we can learn about His character, and behold Him by seeing the wonderful things Scripture reveals to us about Him. So let's move ahead and behold our awesome God!

In the Word

For this week, read the following scripture passages:

Creation Account: Genesis 1:1-11, 26-27
Birth of Jesus: Isaiah 9:6; Matthew 1:18-25; Luke 1:26-2:14
Baptism of Jesus: Matthew 3:13-17; Mark 1:9-13; Luke 3:21-23; John 1:29-34

Questions to Consider

1. What are the three persons that comprise the one Godhead?

2. In the creation account, where do the three persons of God appear?

3. In the account of the birth of Jesus, where do the three persons of God appear?

4. In the story of Jesus' baptism, where do the three persons of God appear?

5. In the above accounts, do the three persons of God work together, and in agreement with one another?

Journal Activity

After reading the text and answering the questions above, write a paragraph in your journal answering the following question: What does the phrase "three-in-one" mean to you?

Decisions for Life

From Scripture, we can see God is a three-in-one being, who consists of God the Father, God the Holy Spirit, and God the Word, and Son, Jesus Christ. The three persons form one God who works out His plan for our lives.

God the Father made the plan of creation, and initiated it by speaking forth the Word. The Holy Spirit is the active agent and powerful force that does what the Father commands, through the Word. Together the three persons of God created the heavens and the earth, and all therein, in six days. On the seventh day, God rested—not because He was tired, but because He wanted to show us "resting" is a good thing, because He knew that, as humans, our bodies needed rest.

God created mankind for relationship with Him. Before Adam and Eve fell into sin, God walked with them in the Garden of Eden. When they ate the forbidden fruit, Adam and Eve's sin broke off their relationship with God, causing them to hide. But God wanted His people, and relationship with them, back so He made a way to conquer the power of sin and eternal death.

The heavenly Father's plan of redemption began with the birth of Jesus. The Holy Spirit, through prophetic words, predicted the coming of God's Son. The Holy Spirit overshadowed Mary, and conceived in her. Through conception, the Word became flesh and dwelt among us in the person of Jesus Christ, God's only begotten Son. Jesus died for our sins, and made a way for mankind to be reconciled to God. Through the work on the cross, God made a way we could be raised up to spend eternity with Him, as adopted sons, in His heavenly household. If we accept (or receive) the work Jesus did on the cross for us, and believe in Him, in God's time and way, He will raise us up to be with Him.

God has a great purpose for building His heavenly household. In 1 Peter 2:9 Peter writes to the church saying, " But you are a chosen generation, a royal priesthood, a holy nation, His own special people, that you may proclaim the praises of Him who called you out of darkness into His marvelous light; (...)." Peter continued saying, "Coming to Him as to a living stone, rejected indeed by men, but chosen by God and precious, you also, as living stones, are being built up a spiritual house, a holy priesthood, to offer up spiritual sacrifices acceptable to God through Jesus Christ." (1 Peter 2:4-5)

All three persons of the Godhead are working toward fulfillment of this purpose, which will come to pass when God's plan is completed, and Jesus comes back again. God's plan WILL be completed; no person can thwart His plan, because of who He is. Behold, our awesome God is three-in-one!

This week make a decision to accept and believe—by faith—that our God is a three-in-one being, consisting of God the Father, The Holy Spirit, and God the Word and Son, Jesus Christ. Also, choose to believe the three persons of the Godhead work together to complete God's plan and purpose.

Like Mary, the mother of Jesus, God has a special plan for your life! He has a great and awesome work He wants to do in—and through—you. So make a decision to step out in faith, and believe God wants you to be part of His kingdom, and His family. He wants to love you throughout eternity! So make a decision to allow God to work out His plan for your life. Begin to step out by establishing a personal relationship with God through daily prayer, and reading His word.

Live the Life

Choose one of the following activities to complete in order to put what you've learned in this lesson into practice:

1. In a Bible concordance, look up 10 scriptures about God the Father, and write down what they say about Him. Then, on your journal page for this lesson, write a paragraph about what you learned about God the Father.

2. Read John, chapter three, and note the characteristics given about the Holy Spirit. What natural force does Jesus use to describe the Holy Spirit? What is the task the Holy Spirit does in this passage? What does it mean to be "born again"? Write a paragraph about these questions, and the Holy Spirit, on the journal page for this lesson.

3. In a Bible concordance, look up 10 scriptures about God's Son, Jesus, and write down what they tell us about Him. Then, on your journal page for this lesson, write a paragraph about what you learned about God's Son, Jesus Christ.

4. Scripture tells us that Jesus came to show us the Father. Glance through the gospels (Matthew, Mark, Luke, John), and write down a list of 10 things Jesus did that shows us the divine

nature and/or power of God. Then, on your journal page for this lesson, write a paragraph explaining how Jesus showed us the Father.

Review, Reflect, and Respond

Spend some time reviewing the lesson. Write down any new things you learned. Also note any ideas, questions, or thoughts you might want to share, or have addressed. Spend some time in Scripture searching for the answers to your questions. If you can't find the answers, set up an appointment with your Pastor or church leader, to have your questions addressed. Our church authority, and teachers, are there to help keep order in God's house, and to teach us about His Word. They are valuable resources for anyone who is serious about learning the Bible, including learning about God. If you are not attending a local church, you can email your questions to me at getrobinu@gmail.com. I will be happy to see if I can find the answers through the resources available to me, including the leaders in my church.

Close in Prayer

Thank God for who He is, and for His attribute of being "three-in-one." Thank Him for sending Jesus to pay the penalty for our sin, to demonstrate God's love, and to show us the Father. Also ask God to reveal Himself to you, so you can get to know Him better. Then approach God with any personal requests you may have.

Lesson 8

God Is our Heavenly Father

"Blessed be the God and Father of our Lord Jesus Christ, (...),
just as He chose us in Him before the foundation of the world,
that we should be holy and without blame before Him in love,
having predestined us to adoption as sons
by Jesus Christ to Himself,
according to the good pleasure of His will,"
--Ephesians 1:3-5

"And because you are sons,
God has sent forth the Spirit of His Son into your hearts,
crying out, 'Abba Father!'"
--Galatians 4:6

"'I will be a Father to you,
and you will be My sons and daughters,'
says the Lord Almighty."
--2 Corinthians 6:18

Open in Prayer

Pray God will reveal His desire to be your loving heavenly Father
to you. Ask Him to show you He can—and will be—a good Father
to you.

If you have never known your natural father, or if you had an abusive natural father, ask God to help you understand He is not like earthly fathers. He does not sin against His family! He will love, and care for you, and your needs. <u>**Note:**</u> **At times, we have difficulty relating to our heavenly Father because of bad relationships with our natural fathers in this life.**

God is love. He accepts us as His children, loves us unconditionally, and will never abandon us. Thank God for making a way we can become His adopted sons and daughters.

Memory Verses

Spend time every day this week working on memorizing the opening Scriptures. It's exciting to know God has predestined us to be adopted as His children! This Scripture is great encouragement to us when our walk with God becomes difficult. Hang on to God's promises, and the cross, when times of suffering and tribulation come upon you. Hebrews 6:19 tells us, "This hope we have [Jesus] as an anchor of the soul, both sure and steadfast, and which enters the Presence behind the veil".

Beginning Activity

Take a few minutes to think about fathers. What is their role, and their responsibilities to their families? On your journal page for this lesson, make a list of characteristics you think a good father should have. Also, if you have a special memory of your father, write a brief paragraph describing it, and telling why it means so much to you. Then pray and thank God for the special memory you have of your father.

Lesson Introduction

Even before the creation of the heaven and earth, God—in His foreknowledge—knew us, and made a plan and purpose for us to fulfill, as we live out our lives. God created us for His pleasure and purpose, because He wanted a people He could call His own, who would love Him in return, with their own free will. God wants us to have relationship with Him. God will not force us to love Him because that is not love! God gets no glory or relationship from a kingdom of robots that are forced to love, and serve Him. Therefore, He left the choice up to us, and He won't go against our choice. Our heavenly Father is the first person of the three-in-one God.

When we are born again by the Holy Spirit, we become new creations in Christ Jesus and children of God. If we continue believing in God and walking with Him throughout our lives, we become sons of God, and have a place in His earthly kingdom and His heavenly household. When born again, we are made acceptable to God by the cleansing power of the blood of Jesus, and the victory Jesus obtained over sin and spiritual death when He died on the cross at Calvary. We are given the righteousness of Christ.

Becoming a member of God's household cannot be achieved in our own human strength and abilities. We cannot earn or work our way to heaven. Our salvation is a free gift, given to us only by the grace of God. We must come to Jesus, and be born again by the Holy Spirit, in order to be saved. In John 14:6 Jesus said, "I am the way, the truth, and the life. No one comes to the Father except through Me."

When we are born again, God becomes our heavenly Father through the gospel. In this lesson, we see how Jesus explains being 'born again' to a man named Nicodemus. Many of you may already be born again, but it's good to be reminded of how we became children of God. It's good to refresh our knowledge of the Bible. It can prepare us for the work God has for us to do. It is important people know that going to church every week, or doing good works, will not get you to heaven. It's only by being born again that we can enter the kingdom of God. It is also important for those who are born again to remember that when we came to Jesus, we came to the cross, just as we were—lost sinners. Accept for the grace of God, go I.

In this world, many false religions offer many wrong paths to many different gods. These people deceive multitudes of others, causing them to be misled down the path to destruction. One of these great myths is "all roads lead to Rome," and there are many paths to god. This is a tragic lie, spread by the evil one and his cohorts, throughout the world. Scripture warns us about taking the correct path saying, "Enter by the narrow gate; for wide is the gate and broad is the way that leads to destruction, and there are many who go in by it. Because narrow is the gate and difficult is the way which leads to life, and there are few who find it." (Matthew 7:13-14) Jesus is the only way to the Father in heaven. (John 14:6) It's vital we share this message with those who have not yet heard it!

It's also vital for Christian believers to know we are God's adopted children, whom He loves with unconditional, unfailing love. It's important we understand who we are in Christ (See Ephesians, chapters 1-3) so we will have confidence in approaching the throne of God, and also when fighting in spiritual battle against evil. We need to stand firm when the flaming darts of the evil one come at us, use the shield of faith with which to quench them, and war with our spiritual sword, which is the Word of God. In fact, we are told we have spiritual armor, God has given us, and we are to put it on. Eph. 6:13-18 says, "Therefore take up the whole armor of God, that you may be able to withstand in the evil day, and having done all, to stand. Stand therefore, having girded your waist with truth, having put on the breastplate of righteousness, and having shod your feet with the preparation of the gospel of peace; above all, taking the shield of faith with which you will be able to quench all the fiery darts of the wicked one. And take the helmet of salvation, and the sword of the Spirit, which is the word of God; praying always with all prayer and supplication in the Spirit, being watchful to this end with all perseverance and supplication for all the saints (…)." Jesus has already won our victory, and all we have to do is stand firm, and above all stand, on the Word of God!

Let's move ahead and learn about being born again and becoming children of the heavenly Father.

In the Word

Read Genesis 1:1-2, 26-31; Genesis 2:1-25; and John 3:1-21. After reading the above passages, answer the questions in the next section.

Questions to Consider

1. In this world, when people create new things, they sometimes become known as the father of their creation. What did God create that He could be called the Father of?

2. Did God have any natural substance (raw material) from which to create His beings?

3. According to the verses in John chapter 3, who is the one doing the conversion/conception in Spiritual new birth?

4. After people are born again, who becomes their Spiritual Father?

5. According to 1 Peter 2:9, we have become God's special people for what purpose?

Journal Activity

On your journal page for this lesson, make a list of your fathers and grandfathers. If they are living, make a list of any needs they may have, whether spiritual, natural, or physical. Also, if you know of anyone who is being abused by their father's bad behavior, put down their father's name and their name, and the needs of both, on your list. Then pray God would divinely intercede, and meet the needs of these people. Pray every day for a week for the people and needs on your list.

Decisions for Life

If you are a father, make a decision to get into God's Word and learn about the role and responsibilities God has given to Christian fathers. If you see areas where you fall short, ask God to help you, and do your best to follow God's guidelines to improve your situation. Also make a decision to walk closer with God, and to be a good example of a Godly father for your family.

If you are not a father or grandfather, make every effort to show appreciation and respect to your father and/or grandfather for the good things they contribute to your life. Perhaps you can get a card or send a special message to encourage the fathers and/or grandfathers in your life. Or perhaps you can cook a special dinner or help them with some chores. Make a decision to show your appreciation for them more often!

In addition to your earthly fathers and grandfathers, make a decision to do something special for your Father in heaven. If you have no earthly fathers or grandfathers in your life, you always have your heavenly Father there with you. Make a decision to express your love and appreciation to Him, and follow through with a special prayer or deed that will bring Him pleasure!

In our daily walk with God, we should endeavor to walk in ways that bring pleasure to Him. Spend some time thinking of new ways to do this, then act upon your ideas. You will bring pleasure to God and be blessed!

Live the Life

Choose one of the following activities to complete in order to put what you've learned from this lesson into practice in your daily life:

1. Take time every day for a week to pray and thank God the Father for the things He does for you.

2. If you know someone who has a special need, or if you have one yourself, pray every day for a week for God to meet the need.

3. On your journal page for this lesson, make a list of some ways you can show appreciation to your husband, father or grandfather. Do one of these things every day for a week to show your love to them.

4. Look up the word "Father" in your Bible concordance. On the journal page for this lesson, list 10 Scripture references for "Father." Then look up the verses and note what they say about God, the heavenly Father.

Review, Reflect, and Respond

Review this week's lesson and write down what you've learned in your journal. Also write down any Scriptures or things God personally revealed to you, as you studied this lesson. Later you can refer to your notes as a reminder of what you've learned.

Close in Prayer

Pray and ask God to show you His loving, Fatherly nature. Thank Him for the things He does in your heart and life. If you are a husband, father, or grandfather, ask God to help you become better in the role He has given you. Also ask Him to show you any areas where you need improvement. When God answers, listen and obey.

God moves in awesome ways in the hearts, homes, and lives of His children. He wants to be included, and to help with every relationship and need. By praying, we invite Him in, and let Him know we want and need His help. If we ask, God will move on our behalf! God is big enough to do the work, even if it takes a miracle! Situations that are impossible for people are, if we ask Him, open invitations for God to come, move, and be glorified!

Lesson 9

God Is the Holy Spirit

"God is Spirit, and those who worship Him
must worship in spirit and truth."
--John 4:24

"Jesus answered and said to him,
'Most assuredly, I say to you,
unless one is born again,
he cannot see the kingdom of God.'"
--John 3:3

"That which is born of flesh is flesh,
and that which is born of the Spirit is spirit."
--John 3:6

"The wind blows where it wishes, and you hear the sound of it,
but cannot tell where it comes from and where it goes.
So is everyone who is born of the Spirit."
--John 3:8

Open in Prayer

Ask God to reveal the Holy Spirit to you this week. Ask Him to help you understand that though the Holy Spirit is invisible, He is a real being, a person of the three-in-one God. Also ask Him to help us understand what the terms "new birth" and "born again" mean. Thank God for the Holy Spirit.

Memory Verses

Spend time this week memorizing the above verses. You may want to write them down on index cards, and carry them with you. Then, if you find yourself waiting for someone, or having a break time at work, you can pull your verses out and spend time memorizing them.

Beginning Activity

In this week's lesson we see how Jesus used the wind to illustrate some characteristics of the Holy Spirit. For the beginning activity, find some small pieces of scrap paper. Cut the paper into pieces no larger than one inch square. Put the pieces of paper on a small plate, and gently blow on them. Watch how they move, and then ask yourself the following questions, and record your answers on the journal page for this lesson:

1. Can we see the wind?
2. Is the wind real; does it exist?
3. How do we know the wind is real?
4. What evidence is there to validate the wind's existence?
5. Is the wind powerful?

Once you've finished writing the answers to the questions down on your journal page, repeat the questions, replacing the word "wind" with "Holy Spirit," and answer the questions again. Notice the similarities between the wind and the Holy Spirit. Then write a paragraph answering the following questions: "Do you think the wind is a good way to illustrate the Holy Spirit? Why or why not?"

Lesson Introduction

In this lesson we learn about the third person of our three-in-one God—The Holy Spirit. In Scripture, John 4:24 says, "God is Spirit, and His worshipers must worship in spirit and truth." According to Unger's Bible Dictionary by Merrill F. Unger[2] (Unger 1957, 1961, 1966, 1967, 1969, 1970, 1971, 1972, 1973, 1974), the word "spirit" is defined as: 1. A term used in the Scriptures generally to denote purely spiritual beings, also the spiritual, immortal part in man. (…). (p. 1043)

God's Word tells us the Holy Spirit is a spiritual being. It also reveals many other things about The Holy Spirit to us. It tells us The Holy Spirit convicts the world of sin, comforts, leads and guides to the truth, and is our helper. The Holy Spirit also gives us spiritual gifts, and does many other tasks.

One day, while ministering to His disciples, Jesus told them He would die, and rise again three days later. Jesus also explained He would be lifted up to Heaven to sit at the right hand of the throne of God. Then, encouraging His disciples, Jesus said, "But because I have said these things to you, sorrow has filled your heart. Nevertheless I tell you the truth. It is to your advantage that I go away; for if I do not go away, the Helper will not come to you; but if I depart, I will send Him to you. And when He has come, He will convict the world of sin, and of righteousness, and of judgment: of sin, because they do not believe in Me; of righteousness, because I go to My Father and you see Me no more; of judgment, because the ruler of this world is judged. (John 16:6-11)

Jesus spoke more about the Holy Spirit's purpose for coming to us, saying, "However, when He, the Spirit of Truth, has come, He will guide you into all truth; for He will not speak on His own authority, but whatever He hears He will speak; and He will tell you things to come. He will glorify Me, for He will take of what is Mine and declare it to you." (John 16:13-14)

In this lesson we look at a few of the attributes of God, The Holy Spirit. We will see The Holy Spirit is an invisible spiritual being, He is powerful, He leads and guides us, He convicts the world of sin, and He brings about new birth, by which we can enter the kingdom of God.

We will also look at a passage of scripture where Jesus teaches a man named Nicodemus about the Holy Spirit, new birth, and seeing the kingdom of God. So get excited, grab your Bible, and let's get in the Word!

In the Word

Open your Bible to the gospel of John, and read John 3:1-21. Then use this passage to answer the questions below.

Questions to Consider

1. What convinced Nicodemus Jesus was from God, and caused him to seek out Jesus for answers to his questions?

2. What reason did Jesus give Nicodemus in order to explain why Nicodemus couldn't see the kingdom of God?

3. What confused Nicodemus about the phrase "born again"?

4. What illustration did Jesus use to teach Nicodemus about the movement of the Holy Spirit?

5. Which person of the Godhead does the work of conversion in new birth or being "born again"?

Journal Activity

Reread the "Welcome" section in the front of this book to find out what a person needs to do in order to be "born again." In your own words, write these instructions on the journal page for this lesson. Review them periodically to refresh your memory. Then, if you meet someone who wants to enter the kingdom of God, you can explain what they need to do, and pray with them.

Decisions for Life

One of the most important decisions you will make in life is to decide what you personally believe about the three persons of the one God. God the Father draws men to Himself, the Holy Spirit convicts them of their sin and shows them their need for God, and the Word and Son of God, Jesus Christ, came to earth to be the way for people to believe, have atonement for their sins, get born again, and be raised up to heaven as adopted sons of God!

What we believe about God, especially about Jesus Christ, will eventually determine our eternal spiritual destination. God tells us Jesus came that whoever believes in Him will not perish but have eternal life. But those who do not believe will not be saved. Therefore, make a decision to get in your Bible and find out who Jesus is, and what He did on your behalf. Then, make another decision to believe in Jesus Christ and the work He accomplished on your behalf!

In John 6:28-29 the people asked Jesus, "What shall we do, that we may work the works of God?" Jesus answered them saying, "This is the work of God, that you believe in Him whom He sent."

If you're born again and have made your decision about eternity, then make a decision to get into God's word regularly, and learn more about

Him. What we believe—God's word or our own ideas—can help or hinder our walk with God. Read God's word, and take time to get to know Him, and develop a personal relationship with Him through daily reading His word and praying. You will get to know Him better, and you will also be blessed!

After making any of the above decisions for your life, write them down on the journal page for this lesson as a reminder for you to follow through, and apply what you've learned to your life.

Live the Life

Choose one of the following activities to apply what you've learned to your daily life:

1. In a Bible concordance, look up ten verses on the Holy Spirit and note what part the Holy Spirit has in God's overall plan. Write down what you learned from the verses on your journal page.

2. Spend 30 minutes reading your Bible. Take note of any passages of scripture that seem to leap off the pages at you. The Holy Spirit quickens passages to our heart when God has a specific message for us. Write down any scriptures you read and you believe God is using to speak directly to your heart, and review them daily for a week. Write these scriptures on the journal page for this lesson. Then note anything God is asking you to do. Be sure to obey what He says to you!

3. If you're already born again, choose a Christian book you would like to read. As you read through it, note anything that seems disturbing, questionable, or not in line with Scripture. Write these things down on the journal page for this lesson.

When we read, the Holy Spirit lets us know if something we come across is not correct, according to Scripture. If you find something questionable, go to your Bible, look it up, and make sure it agrees with Scripture before you believe it. The Holy Spirit warns us about false things so we won't believe the lies the enemy tries to feed us, and Satan, our adversary, cannot easily lead us astray. Satan wants to destroy God's work in our lives, so we must be cautious about what we read, and listen to the Holy Spirit when He warns us.

1. Make a list of people you know need Jesus Christ in their lives. Write the names down on the journal page for this lesson. Then pray that God the Father will draw them, and the Holy Spirit will convict them of their sin, and show them their need for God. Also pray they will choose to believe in Jesus Christ, and be born again. Pray for this list of people every day for a week, and believe God can save them! Behold our awesome God desires that none of them will perish!

Review, Reflect, and Respond

Spend some time reviewing this lesson. Note any new things you've learned about God or anything God has spoken to you. Keep these notes, and periodically refer to them to repeatedly behold the greatness of our awesome God!

Close in Prayer

Thank God for sending the Holy Spirit to earth to do His work. Pray God will help you discern the work of the Holy Spirit in your daily life better. Also pray God will help you see the movement and work of the Holy Spirit in the lives of those around you.

Lesson 10

God Is the Word, the Son, Jesus

"In the beginning was the Word,
and the Word was with God,
and the Word was God."
--John 1:1

"And the Word became flesh and dwelt among us,
and we beheld His glory,
the glory as of the only begotten of the Father,
full of grace and truth."
--John 1:14

"(…), but grace and truth came through Jesus Christ."
--John 1:17

"For in Him dwells all the fullness of the Godhead bodily;"
--Colossians 2:9

Open in Prayer

Ask God to help you understand that Jesus is the Word who became flesh and dwelt among us, and He is God's only begotten Son. The Word became flesh and dwelt among us so Jesus could pay the penalty for our sins and reveal the Father to us. Now we have the Bible, God's written word, through which He reveals His message to us. Take time to thank God for sending His Word and Son, Jesus Christ, to earth for us!

Memory Verses

Spend time every day this week memorizing the opening Scriptures. These are foundational to your understanding the connection between the Old and New Testaments in the Bible. They are also vital to your understanding of Jesus' identity, and why He came to us. Some say Jesus was just a good prophet or a good teacher or simply just a good man. But these verses, and others found in Scripture, confirm Jesus Christ is truly God, the Word who became flesh and dwelt among us, and God's one and only begotten Son.

Beginning Activity

Take a few minutes and write John 1:1-18 on your journal page for this lesson. Then underline the parts of scripture you know speak about Jesus.

Lesson Introduction

For many years Old Testament Prophets spoke about a Messiah who would come from God to rule and reign in Jerusalem. The Jewish people waited with anticipation for God to fulfill His promise because of the cruelty of the Roman rulers reigning over them.

Roman soldiers came to the villages and took food from the people. At one point King Herod, who was appointed by Rome to rule over the Jewish people, sent soldiers to kill the small children because he didn't want the Messiah to come and take his throne. Christians were tortured, crucified, and beheaded for their beliefs in Jesus Christ.

Under another leader, Nero, God's people were put to death in an arena and killed as a form of entertainment for the Roman people. Many Christians, including most of the Apostles and Jesus, were killed by rulers in the Roman Empire. No wonder the Jewish people and early Christian believers wanted their Messiah to come, and rescue them from the hands of the Roman Empire! But God had a different plan.

God sent His one and only begotten Son, Jesus Christ, to deliver all people from the evil consequences of the fall of Adam and Eve in the Garden of Eden. God wanted to deliver all people from the power of sin, and spiritual death. So God set a plan into motion to atone for the sins of people, and to make a way for them to become members of His kingdom, and adopted children in His heavenly household. So the Word of God became flesh and dwelt among us in the body of a human. God's Son, Jesus, was conceived by the Holy Spirit in the womb of a virgin girl named Mary. Mary gave birth to God's Son, Jesus, who was also the coming Messiah. The Messiah, who was expected to come in majesty and power, entered the world as a baby boy!

Though Jesus lived among the Jewish people, many of them did not recognize Him as the Messiah, the Son of God. Because of the people's great dream of the Messiah being a conqueror, and throwing off the yoke of the Roman Empire, many of them did not believe Jesus was the Messiah and Son of God. Though Jesus fulfilled many prophecies, and did many miracles in their midst, many people did not receive Him. But for those who did receive Him, He made a way for them to be reconciled to God, and become adopted children of God.

In the previous lesson, "God is three-in-one," we looked at several Scriptures, proving that "The Word was God, the Word came and dwelt among us, and the Word was Jesus Christ. We also saw a brief Scripture passage of Mary's conception, and the birth of Jesus.

In this lesson we dig a little deeper into these truths, and hopefully expand your knowledge and understanding about Jesus, the Word in flesh, God's only begotten Son. So let's move forward and spend some time in the Word.

In the Word

This week's Bible lesson is taken from the following scripture passages:

Isaiah 9:6-7   Luke 1:26-44   Matt. 1:16-25
Luke 2:1-7   John 1:1-18

The following Biblical account has been paraphrased to help shorten it. I encourage you to read the actual verses for yourself!

God Sends His Son

For years the people of Israel heard God's message by listening to God's prophets, and the priests who read Scripture from the Pentateuch to them. The prophets foretold the coming of a great King, a Messiah, that would rule over the people and bring peace. One of God's prophets, a man named Isaiah, prophesied saying, "For unto us a Child is born, unto us a Son is given; And the government will be upon His shoulder. And His name will be called Wonderful, Counselor, Mighty God, Everlasting Father, Prince of Peace. Of the increase of His government and peace there will be no end, (...)." (Isaiah 9:6-7) Isaiah and several other prophets brought news about the Messiah, along with other messages and promises from God.

God's people were waiting and watching for the promised Messiah who would someday rule over them. The people built up a perception of the Messiah coming in glory, and delivering them from the Roman Government.

But God sent His Son, Jesus Christ—the Messiah, to earth in the form of a baby who was born in a stable in Bethlehem. Scripture tells us:

"Now in the sixth month the angel Gabriel was sent by God to a city of Galilee named Nazareth, to a virgin betrothed to a man whose name was Joseph, of the house of David. The virgin's name was Mary. And having come in, the angel said to her, 'Rejoice, highly favored one, the Lord is with you; blessed are you among women!' But when she saw him, she was troubled at his saying, and considered what manner of greeting this was. Then the angel said to her, 'Do not be afraid, Mary, for you have found favor with God. And behold, you will conceive in your womb and bring forth a Son, and shall call His name JESUS. He will be great, and will be called the Son of the Highest; and the Lord God will give Him the throne of His father David. And He will reign over the house of Jacob forever, and of His kingdom there will be no end.'

Then Mary said to the angel, 'How can this be, since I do not know a man?' And the angel answered and said to her, 'The Holy Spirit will come upon you, and the power of the Highest will overshadow you; therefore, also, that Holy One who is to be born will be called the Son of God (...) For with God nothing will be impossible.' Then Mary said, 'Behold the maidservant of the Lord! Let it be to me according to your word.' And the angel departed from her." (Luke 1:26-38)

When Mary told her future husband, Joseph, what had happened, He had in mind to divorce her quietly because he did not want to expose Mary to public disgrace. After Joseph considered this, an angel of the Lord appeared to him in a dream and said, "Joseph, son of David, do not be afraid to take Mary home as your wife because what is conceived in her is from the Holy Spirit. She will give birth to a Son, and you are to give Him the name Jesus because He will save His people from their sins." When Joseph woke up, he took Mary home as his wife, but he had no union with her until she gave birth. (Matthew 1:18-25)

During the time of Mary's pregnancy, a ruler named Caesar Augustus issued a decree that a census should be taken of the entire Roman world. Because of this decree, Joseph and his expectant wife, Mary, had to travel to Bethlehem to be counted. While in Bethlehem Mary gave birth to her firstborn, a son, and wrapped Him in cloths and placed Him in a manger because there was no room for them in the inn. (Luke 2:1-7)

Joseph named the baby "Jesus," and God's Son, the Messiah, had entered the world. Jesus grew up, and eventually gave His life as a sacrifice to pay the penalty for all the sins of mankind—from beginning until the end—and He became the way for them to become adopted children of God.

Jesus will return someday to rule and reign over all the earth, from Jerusalem, for a thousand years. He will turn the whole world over to the Heavenly Father. Then God's adopted sons will rule and reign with Him throughout eternity as kings and priests.

As He promised, God did send His Son, the Word in flesh, into the world. But because the peoples' perceptions of His coming were so distorted, they did not recognize Him, and many people did not believe or receive Him. They expected a King in glory, majesty, and splendor, but received their King as an infant, who, after birth, began His life lying in a manger. John 1:10 tells us, "He was in the world, and the world was made through Him, and the world did not know Him."

As God's children living in this world today, we must be careful not to make the same mistake. We must not build, in our minds, an unchangeable, firm perception of God or Jesus so we refuse to change. Jesus is coming again, and we don't want to miss Him because He doesn't fit into the perception we have constructed in our minds. We must be "open and teachable" just in case God has different plans!

Questions to Consider:

Search the story "God Sends His Son" or the scripture passages listed above to find the answers to the following questions:

1. In John 1:1-17 who became flesh and dwelt among us?

2. Who was the human man through which the Word of God came to us?

3. What virgin girl allowed God to work through her and thereby became the mother of God's Son?

4. According to John 1:12 who did Jesus give the right to become children of God?

5. Who is the Father of Jesus?

6. Is it always easy to step out in faith and do what God wants you to do?

7. Is it always necessary to be obedient and do what God asks, even if it seems strange to us?

Decisions for Life

In John chapter 14, Jesus comforts His disciples after telling them He wouldn't be here on earth with them much longer. Jesus explained that He would die on the cross, be resurrected three days later, and be lifted up to the right hand of the throne of God, His Father, in heaven. Jesus also said He was going to prepare a place for them in heaven. During this time Jesus said, "I am the way and the truth and the life. No one comes to the Father except through Me." (John 14:6)

The gospel of Matthew tells about two gates that people can choose to go through as they live out their lives on earth, and the gate they choose will determine where they spend eternity. Jesus said, "Enter by the narrow gate; for wide is the gate and broad is the way that leads to destruction, and there are many who go in by it. Because narrow is the gate and difficult is the way which leads to life, and there are few who find it." (Matthew 7:13-14)

In John 10:9 Jesus says, "I am the door. If anyone enters by Me, he will be saved, and will go in and out and find pasture." In essence Jesus is telling us that to have eternal life in heaven, we must believe in Him, and accept the work He did, in our behalf, on the cross at Calvary. We must follow the path He has laid before us, and enter through Him— The Narrow Gate.

If you haven't already done so, make a decision to go down the narrow path, and enter into heaven through being born again, and through faith in Jesus Christ and the work He did on the cross. Ask God to forgive you of all your sins; then ask Jesus to come and live in your heart, and be your Lord and Savior. To be "Lord" means He becomes our "resident Boss."

For those who have already been born again, consider your perception of God, including His Son Jesus, and the Word of God. Do you have a perception of God that is limited, and makes Him look smaller— and less powerful—than He really is? Do you have a true picture of who Jesus is? Do you believe He is the Messiah, the Son of God? Is your perception so firmly planted in your mind that you are unwilling to change it if God should decide to move in a different way than expected? Today, make a decision to get into God's word and find out the truth about these matters. Also, make a decision to allow God His way—to open or change your perceptions—should He desire to do so. God is so much more than we can ever place in a box, in our finite minds!

If you have a misconception of God or His Son, Jesus, make a decision to get into the Bible and discover the truth. Then, receive—by faith— what the Word of God says! God is three-in-one, and Jesus is not a mere man, or simply a good teacher, or only a prophet. He is the Word of God, God's Son, and in Him is the fullness of the Deity! Jesus is God. John 1:1, our memory verse, says, "In the beginning was the Word, and the Word was with God, and the Word was God." John 1:14-17 tells us that Jesus is the Word. Therefore, Jesus is God.

Another misconception people have is that "Christianity" and "Religion" are the same. That is not true! "Religion" is peoples' attempts to try to reach up to God, by works done with their own strengths and abilities, with the goal of somehow getting to God through their own effort. "Christianity," as we have seen in this Bible study, is God's way of coming to man, and reconciling them to Himself. It is not an act from peoples' effort, but a belief in Jesus Christ, God's Son, and a new birth, a work done by God's Holy Spirit, through what Jesus has accomplished upon the cross.

If you have a misconception about "Christianity" and "Religion" make a decision to learn about the differences between to two, and to accept and receive what is true.

Once a person has been born again by the Holy Spirit, they do works God has planned in advance for them to do. However, their motive for doing the works is a love for God. It is not to reach God by earning their way to heaven. These works are done from a grateful heart that wants to obey God, and do what He asks, because they love Him, and they recognize the wonderful things He has done for them! The works people do before they get born again are as filthy rags to God. They count nothing towards earning God's free gift of salvation. People simply cannot make their own way to heaven, regardless of how good they seem to be, or think they are, because they do not measure up to God's standards of acceptability. Only the righteousness of Christ, given to those who are born again through receiving and believing, will be accepted by God.

Because of their obedience, God used Joseph and Mary to accomplish His great miraculous work! God still uses His children in today's world by working through them to complete His miracles. These miracles are done—not by human strength or ability—but by the power of God working through them. So if you hear God asking you to do something, make a decision to believe, obey, and watch, to see what miraculous thing God will do through you!

Live the Life

Complete one of the following activities to put what you've learned from this lesson into practice:

1. How do you think you would respond if an angel suddenly appeared before your eyes? Would you be fearful? Would you think you're having a dream or vision? Write a paragraph about how you think you would respond to this surprise.

2. If you were in Mary's place—pregnant with God's child—how would you feel about having to tell your future husband you were with child? How do you think the people of Mary's time period would have treated her when they found out about the pregnancy? Write a paragraph about your thoughts on your journal page for this lesson.

3. If you were engaged to marry someone and they suddenly told you they were going to have a child that was conceived by God the Holy Spirit, in which you had no part of the conception, how would you react? What would you think? Write a paragraph responding to the situation on your journal page.

4. Who do you believe Jesus is? Write a paragraph on your journal page explaining this.

5. On your journal page, make a list of differences and similarities between "Christianity" and "Religion." Write a two-or-more-paragraph paper contrasting the two beliefs.

6. Do you think God could work through you to do a miracle? Or do you have a testimony where God has done this? Write a paragraph about your thoughts on your journal page.

Review, Reflect, and Respond

Spend a few minutes reviewing and reflecting on what you've learned this week. Write a brief paragraph about your thoughts on your journal page. If you have any questions about this lesson, write them down as well, and research the Bible to see if you can find the answers. If you can't find the answers, then ask your Pastor or email me, and I will see if I can find them for you with the resources at my disposal.

Close in Prayer

Thank God for sending the Word, His Son, Jesus Christ, down to earth to save us from our sins, to reveal God to us, and to be the way for us to become adopted sons of God, so we can spend eternity in God's heavenly household.

Lesson 11

God Knows Everything!

"O Lord, You have searched me and known me.
You know my sitting down and my rising up;
You understand my thought afar off.
You comprehend my path and my lying down,
and are acquainted with all my ways.
For there is not a word on my tongue,
but behold, O Lord, You know it altogether."
--Psalm 139:1-4

"The woman then left her waterpot,
went her way into the city,
and said to the men,
"Come, see a Man who told me all things that I ever did.
Could this be the Christ?"
--John 4:28-29

Open in Prayer

As you open this lesson with a prayer, ask God to show you how well He knows you, and what He desires you learn from this lesson. Pray that God will reveal how much He loves you! Praise Him for His ability to know everything!

Memory Verses

Spend time this week planting the opening verses in your memory bank. The more scripture we know, the more God will reveal it to us in our time of need.

Beginning Activity

Can you remember a time when it seemed like your spouse or friend knew what you were going to say even before you said it? Or do you remember a time when both of you came up with the same idea or thought at the same time? If so, write a brief paragraph on your journal page explaining how the experience made you feel. Did you wonder how the other person knew what you were thinking?

Psalm 139:4 tells us, "For there is not a word on my tongue, but behold, O Lord, You know it altogether." How do you feel, knowing God knows the words on your tongue even before you speak them? Write a brief response explaining how you feel knowing that God knows what you are going to say before you even say it.

God knows everything! We can't even understand our own thoughts and actions, let alone those of the people around us. How can people even think we could be gods or be like God? God is far above us, and He knows everything. Behold, our God is indeed an awesome God!

In this lesson we will look at an attribute of God called "omniscience" which means "all-knowing." *Webster's New World Dictionary with Student Handbook, Concise Edition, by World Publishing Company*[3] (1974) defines it, "(...) knowing all things,—the Omniscient, God (p. 521).

Do you remember Jonah from last week's lesson? God knew exactly where Jonah was hiding even though the prophet ran away, and tried to hide from Him.

In this lesson we learn about a Samaritan woman who experienced God's omniscience, as she spoke with Jesus. She was amazed to find out Jesus knew all about her, when she did not even know who He was.

Jesus is the Son of God, and the fullness of the Deity is in Him. Colossians 2:9 tells us, "For in Him dwells the fullness of the Godhead bodily; and you are complete in Him, who is the head of all principality and power."

So let's move ahead and see what happened when a Samaritan woman encountered the Son of God, and experienced His "omniscience."

In the Word

For this week's lesson, read John 4:1-30. After reading the passage, use your Bible to answer the questions below. The more you dig into God's Word, the more you can learn.

Questions to Consider

1. What did Jesus first ask of the woman at the well?

2. What did the woman say in response to Jesus' request?

3. In John 4:10 what did Jesus mean when He used the phrase "living water"?

4. What did Jesus tell the woman about herself in John 4:17?

5. What did Jesus reveal to the Samaritan woman in John 4:26?

6. In John 4:28-29 when the woman left her water pot and went to the city, what two things did she say to the men?

7. What happened as a result of the Samaritan woman's sharing of her testimony with others?

Journal Activity

For your journal activity, choose to write a paragraph about one of the following:

1. Reflect on a time when God touched your life. Do you have a testimony of an encounter with God—when He deeply touched your heart?

2. Have you experienced God's omniscience during your walk with Him? What would you think if a complete stranger came up to you, and suddenly started telling you about your past life?

3. Have you found yourself in a situation when a person, who normally didn't associate with you because of prejudice, suddenly struck up a pleasant conversation with you?

4. Why do you think Jesus brought up the subject of living water?

Decisions for Life

In this lesson we learned about God's omniscience. We have also seen instances in scripture where people were prejudice against the opposite gender or a certain sect of people, because of the differences between them. Make a decision to examine your heart to see if you have any prejudices towards others hidden inside. If you do, make a decision to repent, and ask God forgive you and to help you change. Then leave the prejudices behind, and move forward in a cleansed and changed life.

If you find you want to hide things, or even yourself, from God, know that because of His omniscience, God already knows these things. It is impossible to hide anything from God. If you try to hide sin from God, make a decision to confess it to Him, ask for forgiveness, and repent by turning away from the sin. Know God will forgive you, and you can be cleansed, and press on in a new beginning, as you continue to walk with God.

In this lesson we've learned how well God knows each one of us. But how well do we know Him? Make a decision to spend more time in relationship with God, so you can get to know Him better. Consider giving God all your troubles so He can fight for you. Let Him pour a fresh flow of His Spirit, forgiveness, life, and love into your heart. Let God do all He desires in and through you. Romans 5:5 tells us, "Now hope does not disappoint, because the love of God has been poured out in our hearts by the Holy Spirit who was given to us." God is the only one who can change and heal people, and He does it from the inside out because He knows everything! Behold, our awesome God!

Live the Life

Complete one of the activities below to apply this week's lesson to your daily life:

1. Spend at least 15 minutes every day for a week in prayer. During this prayer time, ask God to help you get to know Him better.

2. Read Psalm 139, and write down what it says that God knows about you. Then spend some time every day for a week meditating and considering how much God knows about you.

3. Is there an area in your life in which you need God to help you overcome? On your journal page for this lesson write a prayer, God asking for His help in this area. Then pray this prayer to God every day for a week, requesting His divine intervention in this circumstance.

4. As you consider how well God knows you, make an attempt to become more aware of His presence in your life. Periodically take a five-minute break in your day to thank God for being there, and for His omniscience, because you are in His hands as you walk through the days He has fashioned for you.

5. If you can remember something special God has done in your life, write about it on your journal page for this lesson. Then share your testimony with someone who needs encouragement and support to get through a difficult time in their life. If that person needs to know God, spend some time telling him/her about Him. Then pray for that person and his or her needs.

Review, Reflect, and Respond

Take a few minutes to review this lesson. Then, on your journal page for this lesson, write down three things you've learned. Review your journal pages periodically to behold our awesome God.

Close in Prayer

Thank God for His omniscience, and for always being there for us. Ask Him to continue to reveal Himself to you. Also ask Him to help you overcome any prejudice or sin in your life. God wants us to love everyone, including our enemies. The Holy Spirit can help us do this by giving us the ability, and the power to overcome circumstances, and to love God and others—even our enemies!

Lesson 12

God Is the Source of Life

"For as the Father has life in Himself,
so He has granted the Son to have life in Himself."
--John 5:26

"For as the Father raises the dead and gives life to them,
even so the Son gives life to whom He will."
--John 5:21

"The Spirit of God has made me,
and the breath of the Almighty gives me life."
--Job 33:4

"And the Lord God formed man of the dust of the ground,
and breathed into his nostrils the breath of life;
and man became a living being."
--Genesis 2:7

Open in Prayer

Ask God to show you what He wants you to learn from this lesson. Also pray for any person you know needs healing or the provision of food, shelter, or other basic needs. Then ask God for any needs you may have.

Memory Verses

Spend time this week learning the memory verses for this lesson. Write them on index cards and carry them with you. Whenever you have a short break in your schedule or find yourself waiting for some reason, use that time to plant the verses in your heart and mind.

Beginning Activity

If you could create a person, what would he/she look like? Would they be tall or short, thin or overweight? What color would their eyes, hair and skin be? Would they be young or old, or happy or sad? What would their occupation be, and what tools would they carry with them as they worked? What kind of foods would they like? What hobbies would they have? Think about these questions and write the answers on your journal page for this lesson.

After compiling your list, write out a brief character sketch of your person on the journal page and/or draw a picture of them. You can draw your character in a complex sketch or a simple cartoon, but please don't resort to the "stickmen" types of drawings because to draw them doesn't require much thought process.

Don't worry if your drawing doesn't turn out perfect, because the experience and planning of characterizing your person will help you understand that the task of creation is extremely complex. Yet these simple drawings don't even scratch the surface of the work God did when He created the heavens and earth, including men and women. Even with all of our knowledge and technology, the scientists of today can't understand many areas of our human body, and how they function. All of the evidence in creation points to a divine being, a master designer and crafter, the one true, living God—our God, Yahweh.

Lesson Introduction

In this lesson we look at God's attribute of being "the Source of life." We will briefly look at God's creation of the heavens and earth. Then we will narrow our focus to the creation of man and woman. We will see that God is the Source of all life! So let's move forward and get in the Word.

In the Word

For this lesson read the following scripture passages: (1) Genesis 1:1-28, (2) Genesis 2:7-8 and (3) Genesis 2:18-25. As you read through these sections notice how many times God spoke forth living beings. God is indeed the Source of life!

Questions to Consider:

1. According to Genesis 1:20 what two groups of living creatures did God create?

2. What does Scripture tell us God created in Genesis 1:24?

3. According to Genesis 1:27 what two beings did God create?

4. According to Genesis 2:7, God made man from the dust of the earth and then he breathed into his nostrils the breath of_____ and man became a living being.

5. According to Genesis 2:21-25 what did God use to create woman?

6. Where did God get the dust from which He made man?

Journal Activity

Choose one of the following items below and write a paragraph in your journal about it:

1. Take some time and look up the word "life" in two or more dictionaries. Then try to write out your own understanding of the definition of "life."

2. Take some time to look up ten verses about "life" in your Bible. Make notes about what each verse says. Then write a brief summary of what you learned. If you have a concordance, it will help you find the verses about life. If you don't have a concordance but you have the Internet, you can go to www.biblegateway.com and use their search tool for finding verses about life.

3. Take a nature walk somewhere in your area. As you walk, observe the sights, and note several different types of living creatures that you see. Then pray and thank God for the living creatures, and the gift of life. On your journal page, write down any special things God revealed to you as you completed this activity.

Decisions for Life

As we have learned in this lesson, God is the Source of life. Make a decision to accept His word as the authority of how everything came into existence. Our Christian walk is a walk of faith. We don't always have all of the detail. But by faith, we trust God that His word is truth.

The Holy Spirit, which dwells within us as believers, confirms to our heart that what we read in God's Word is truth. The Holy Spirit leads and guides us into all truth. People can rationalize, reason, and do research to try and find out the origin of mankind. But in Genesis, the Bible tells us the beginning and origin of man. Yet some people may never believe God's word until they face Him at the white throne judgment. Then they will know what the Bible says is true. Unfortunately, it will be too late for them!

Live the Life

Complete one of the following activities in order to put what you've learned from this lesson into practice in your daily life:

1. On your journal page for this lesson, make a list of some of the creatures God created. Note some of the differences distinguishing one creature from another. Take some time to appreciate the differences in all of God's creations, including man and woman.

2. Pick one category of God's creatures (for example: fish, birds, cattle, etc.). Then look up the category in an Encyclopedia or Field Guide. List the names and distinguishing features of ten species in your category. Note how God made each one with special defense and/or survival methods. Then choose one example from your list, and write a paragraph explaining how God made this creature unique.

3. Take some extra time this week to spend with the people God has put in your life for you to love. Make a list of some of these people who are special to you. Write down one way you could show each person on your list how much you appreciate them. Then get busy and do the things on your list.

    Note: Too often we take for granted those closest to us, and don't appreciate the things they contribute to make our life more meaningful. Also, we frequently forget or don't take time to show them how much we appreciate them. For this assignment, make a special effort to show your loved ones you do appreciate them, and what they bring into your life.

4. Look back on your days past, and remember an event or person God used to teach you how precious life can be. Perhaps you had a family member in serious condition in the hospital. Or perhaps you lost touch with a special person God later brought back into your life. After remembering, write a paragraph telling about the situation, and what finally made you realize the high value of life.

Review, Reflect, and Respond

Take some time to review and reflect on this week's lesson. Then respond by writing a paragraph in your journal telling what God has taught you about life from this lesson.

Close in Prayer

Thank God for giving you the gift of life, and for creating all the creatures and people around you for your enjoyment. If you know of others who need healing, pray for them. Behold, our awesome God is the Source of life and health, and He wants to give these things to His people!

Lesson 13

Review Activity

"One thing I have desired of the Lord,
that will I seek:
That I may dwell in the house of the Lord
all the days of my life,
to behold the beauty of the Lord,
and to inquire in His temple.
--Psalm 27:4

"for in Him we live and move and have our being,
as also some of your own poets have said,
'For we are also His offspring.'"
--Acts 17:28

Open in Prayer

Ask God to help you get a true vision of who He is, and to help you trust Him more. Also ask God to help increase your faith, as we can all use more faith. Thank Him for the opportunity to get to know Him better.

Memory Verses

Spend some time this week memorizing the verses above. It is my prayer that these verses will be the lifelong cry of our hearts.

Beginning Activity

This week's beginning activity is to gather your Bible, a couple of pencils, an eraser, and your materials from the last 12 weeks of this Bible Study. You will need these to complete the review activity.

Lesson Introduction

The review activity for this week is to complete the crossword puzzle on the following pages. This puzzle is a review of all of the previous lessons, and contains material from each one. You can refer to your book and notes to help you. The review activity should be a fun challenge, designed to help you remember what you've learned.

As you work on the puzzle, consider it an "overview" of all we've learned about God. When you see all of characteristics of God at once, it will give you a chance to "behold" Him. He is worthy of all our praise, just because of who He is!

In the Word

Your time in the word this week will be the time you spend looking up answers to fill in the crossword puzzle.

Questions to Consider

Your questions this week are the clues in the puzzle. When you finish the puzzle, you will have completed your time in the Word segment. You can find the puzzle solution in the "Awesome Answers" section in the back of this book.

Crossword Puzzle Review Activity:

Behold Our Awesome God!

Crossword Puzzle Clues

Across:

4 - The three _____ of the Godhead are God the Father, God the Son (Jesus), and the Holy Spirit.

8 - God _____ His love for us by sending Jesus to atone for our sins.

9 - God provides _____, love, meaning, purpose, and lasting rewards in life.

11 - _____ of God's existence surrounds us in creation.

12 - God has the _____ to resurrect the dead.

14 - We _____ God through reading His Word, prayer, and personal encounters with Him.

17 - God becomes our heavenly Father when we are _____ again.

19 - We can see evidence that _____ working in someone's heart by the change in his or her life.

20 - Jesus is the _____ in flesh that dwelt among us. (John 1:1-17)

22 - God also wants us to love one _____.

24 - God wants us to love _____ above everything else.

25 - The Samaritan woman told the people about her _____ with Jesus.

26 - God confronts us about our sin with a motive of _____ us to Him.

27 - Jesus gave those who _____ Him the right to become children of God.

28 - Jesus told the Samaritan woman that He was the _____ to come.

29 - After witnessing a miracle, King Nebuchadnezzar said, "There is no other God who can _____ like this."

30 - God's perfectly planned design is seen in the pathways of the _____.

Down:

1 - Many people came to _____ in Jesus because the Samaritan woman shared her testimony.

2 - God highly values the _____ of people.

3 - The Lord Most High is _____. (Psalm 47:2 NKJV)

5 - Jesus prepared the way for us to become _____ sons of God.

6 - Now God's dwelling place is in the _____ of His people.

7 - Jesus was _____ in Mary's womb by the Holy Spirit.

10 - God's attribute of "_____ everything" is called omniscience.

13 - God is a _____ God.

15 - God's attribute of omnipresence is His ability to be _____ at once.

16 - God is _____. (1 John 4:8)

18 - God wants a personal, one-on-one _____ with us.

21 - God is the _____ of life.

23 - God _____ all of my ways and still loves me.

25 - God is _____ in one.

Decisions for Life

This week make a decision to continue doing personal Bible Study time, and keep walking with God, even after this study is over. Your Bible is a great place to learn about God. Also, there are many other resources available to help you learn more about God, and living the Christian life. Some of these include Bible dictionaries, encyclopedias, commentaries, maps and other books written about the Bible or Christian living.

Live the Life

As you continue your walk with God and learn more about Christian living, don't forget to put what you learn into practice in your life. Knowledge about God is not enough. You need to put the knowledge to use before it will bear fruit in your life.

Review, Reflect, and Respond

After you finish the review activity, reflect and write a response in your journal to the question: "How did this overall study help or inspire me to "Behold our awesome God?""

Close in Prayer

Thank God for the opportunity He has given us to spend time in His Word, learning more about Him. Thank Him for being the Source of life, and for all His other attributes! Thank Him for being your Lord and Savior.

Awesome Answers

Lesson 1

1. He wanted the people to bow down and worship His image of gold.

2. The three Hebrew men were commanded by Yahweh not to bow down and worship idols. They wanted to obey their God over their king.

3. They were bound and put in a fiery furnace.

4. The angel of the Lord came into the fire, unbound them and protected them for as long as they were in the furnace.

5. "There is no other God who can deliver like this."

Lesson 2

1. To hide by the Brook Cherith

2. God commanded the ravens to bring Elijah food.

3. A widow at Zarephath

4. God created and/or multiplied the flour and oil so the widow could have enough to feed Elijah, her son, and herself for many days.

5. He raised up the widows son after the son had died.

Lesson 3

1. Go to Nineveh and cry out against the wickedness in that city.

2. Jonah boarded a ship going to Tarshish to flee from God.

3. Yes. God always knew where Jonah was.

4. The Lord sent out a great wind, and there was a mighty tempest on the sea so that the ship was about to be broken up. When the sailors threw Jonah overboard, the Lord had a big fish swallow Him. God kept Jonah in the belly of the fish for three days, until Jonah finally repented and decided to obey God after all.

5. That the souls of all people, even the wicked, are more important than the plant.

Lesson 4

1. David wanted to build a temple for God.

2. David had shed too much human blood.

3. David's son, Solomon

4. Solomon ruled over God's people; He also built the temple for God.

5. God's presence was too big to dwell in a temple made by human hands.

Lesson 5

1. David sent for her and slept with her.

2. David killed her husband, Uriah

3. That he was living in sin.

4. He deserved to die.

5. David confessed his sin, and the Lord put his sin away. However, David still had to face the consequences of his sin.

Lesson 6

1. Jesus Christ

2. A. The Holy Spirit, B. Jesus

3. To come and save the world from sin, and to give eternal life to those who believe and receive Him.

4. He had risen from the dead.

5. How much God loved us.

Lesson 7

1. God the Father, The Holy Spirit, and Jesus—The Word in Flesh, and God's only begotten Son

2. The Father makes the plan and speaks it out. The Father speaks through the Word, Jesus. The Holy Spirit was hovering over the face of the waters.

3. God, the Holy Spirit, conceived the child. Jesus was the child. The Father made the plan, spoke the commands, and announced the birth of His Son.

4. Jesus is in the water getting baptized, The Father speaks from heaven concerning His Son (confirming and encouraging), and the Holy Spirit descended from heaven like a dove, and remained on Jesus (confirming Christ).

5. Yes, all three are in agreement, working toward a single purpose.

Lesson 8

1. The whole creation including men, women, and all the living creatures

2. No.

3. The Holy Spirit

4. God the Father

5. To proclaim the praises of Him who called you out of darkness into His marvelous light.

Lesson 9

1. Seeing the signs Jesus did

2. Nicodemus had not been born again.

3. Nicodemus did not understand the difference between natural birth and spiritual birth. He did not understand how someone could be "born again" by the Holy Spirit.

4. The wind

5. The Holy Spirit

Lesson 10

1. The Word of God

2. Jesus

3. Mary

4. To those who received Him, and were born of God

5. God, by conception through the Holy Spirit

6. No. It can be very difficult.

7. Yes. Very important.

Lesson 11

1. "Give me a drink."

2. "How is it that You, being a Jew, ask a drink from me, a Samaritan woman?"

3. Life, eternal life

4. She had no husband.

5. He was the Messiah.

6. A. "Come see a man who told me all things I ever did."
   B. "Could this be the Christ?"

7. The men she spoke with went to see Jesus. Because of her testimony many of the Samaritans in that city believed in Him.

Lesson 12

1. Creatures of the waters, birds of the air

2. Cattle, creeping things, beast of the earth

3. Man and woman

4. Life

5. A rib from Adam

6. He created it when He created the earth

Lesson 13—Review Activity:

Crossword Puzzle Solution:

Behold Our Awesome God!

My Personal Journal

Lesson 1:

Lesson 2:

Lesson 3:

Lesson 4:

Lesson 5:

Lesson 6:

Lesson 7:

Lesson 8:

Lesson 9:

Lesson 10:

Lesson 11:

Lesson 12:

Lesson 13:

Teacher-Leader's Guide

Teacher-Leader's Guide

About This Study

"Behold Our Awesome God!" is a 13-week Bible study on the attributes of God, and on how God intervenes in the lives of His people. It shows Scriptural accounts to help illustrate God's attributes in action, as He intervenes in the desperate circumstances in the lives of these people. The attributes of God we study in this book are as follows:

God is: Awesome, All-sufficient, everywhere present, big, personal, love, three-in-one, the heavenly Father, the Holy Spirit, the Word and Son—Jesus, All-knowing, and the Source of life.

Learning about God is learning the foundational truths of the Christian life! God is the Beginning and the End, the Alpha and the Omega. For the Christian, God is our all-in-all!

How can this study be used?

"Behold Our Awesome God!" can be used in many Bible study situations. The 13-week format allows for the study to coincide with a quarter of Sunday School, in a church setting. It can also be used for individual and small group Bible studies. The activities in each lesson provide ample material with variety, and thought-provoking questions, to use as discussion-starters. *"Behold Our Awesome God!"* also provides for memorization of scripture, reflection and response in journal activities and other ways,

and activities demonstrating how God's Word can be applied in our daily lives. It also encourages each student to cultivate their own personal relationship with Jesus, by daily reading the Word and praying.

"Behold Our Awesome God!" can be a personal Bible study, completed by one or more individuals in a home or private setting. Each lesson is to be completed in one week. The scripture memorization will help the students grow in their learning of God's word. The Review, Reflect, and Respond segment will encourage the students to review the lesson, reflect on what they learned, and respond by doing an activity. It will encourage individual thinking, and create memorable experiences, to help plant the lesson firmly in the student's mind.

"Behold Our Awesome God!" will also work for small group Bible Studies. The format for small groups can be as versatile as the leaders of each group. One format could be starting the study with an Introduction night in which the materials are handed out, the schedules and rules are stated, the people are introduced to one another, and the first lesson is assigned. Each student should do their work at home so they can have the necessary time to read through the lesson, do the assignments, and work on the scripture-memory. The student should then take their completed work to the next group meeting, where the teacher can go over the lesson, answer questions, have discussion and prayer time, and assign the next week's lesson. Each teacher-leader can establish his or her group schedule and activities.

"Behold Our Awesome God!" can also be used in a Sunday School setting. As in the previous study situations, the lessons should be completed by the students at home. The Sunday School periods can be used for lesson introductions, assigning homework, class discussion, answering questions, praise time, prayer time, and even fellowship time. Week 1 should be a time of introductions and assigning the first lesson. Week 2 should go over the Week 1 work, and then assign the Week 2 lesson. Each of the following lessons should continue the same format. Sunday

School teachers can choose the items they want to include from the lessons, so that they use their time wisely. Times for prayer, praise and worship, and sharing can also be added depending on the allotment of time each teacher has for his/her class.

My previous book *"HEART to heart A Discipleship and Mentoring Plan"* offers teacher-leaders a wealth of ideas and information to help them with their small groups or classes. It was written as a companion book to the HEART to heart Bible study books. *Behold Our Awesome God* is the first in a series of Bible studies God has put on my heart to write.

Goals and Purpose

"Behold Our Awesome God!" was created to help enable any Christian believer, teacher or not, to disciple and share God's word with others. In the Great Commission, in Matthew 28:16-20, Jesus commands His people to go and make disciples of all nations, baptizing them in the name of the Father, Son, and Holy Spirit, and to teach them everything He had commanded them. The HEART to heart books are designed to help believers work to fulfill this Great Commission by providing them instruction, tools, and encouragement. Only God can work in the hearts and lives of people, planting His word as a teacher-leader speaks it out. Only God can save, heal, and restore broken people. But He chooses to use His children, as instruments, to help in the process. What a privilege it is to be a part of God's great plan!

Some goals for this Bible Study include:

1. Teaching others about God and His work in the lives of people.

2. Encouraging believers to spend time with God daily, reading His Word, and praying, to establish a personal, one-on-one relationship with God.

3. Encouraging students to become members of a local church in the universal body of Christ.

4. Encouraging students to love God above all things.

5. Encouraging students to love others as themselves.

6. Helping students see that God truly cares, even about the smallest details in their lives.

To the Teacher-Leader

Thank You for deciding to teach *"Behold Our Awesome God!"* As a teacher, I want to encourage and help you as much as I can. Therefore, I've included this Teacher-Leader guide. In these pages you will find additional helps, and ideas for leading your group.

Teaching God's word is an honor and privilege, and with it comes great responsibility and great joy! In writing the book of Timothy, the Apostle Paul admonishes this young pastor to "Let no one despise your youth, but be an example to the believers in word, in conduct, in love, in spirit, in faith, in purity. Till I come, give attention to reading, to exhortation, to doctrine. Do not neglect the gift that is in you; which was given you by prophecy with the laying on of hands of the eldership. Meditate on these things; give yourself entirely to them, that your progress may be evident to all. Take heed to yourself and to the doctrine. Continue in them, for in doing this you will save both yourself and those who hear you." (1 Timothy 4:12-16) I believe these words were also meant for Bible teachers. As you teach, know others will listen to your words and also watch your actions, to see if you really believe, and apply what you teach to your life. In saying this, I'm not trying to deter you or put extra stress on you. I only wish to encourage and inform you, to help you become the best teacher you can be!

God calls teachers, and equips them to minister to Christian believers, to equip them for Christian service and for spreading His word to others. But teachers are not the only ones given this responsibility. God has established a five-fold ministry in His church which consists of Pastors, Teachers, Prophets, Apostles (Missionaries), and Evangelists. In addition, God has commanded His disciples to go and make disciples of all nations. God wants all of His people to share His Word, and testimonies of the work He has done in their lives with others. God doesn't want people to perish in the lake of fire, as we see in the closing chapters of the Book of Revelation.

Though God's heart desires for all to come to saving grace, the reality is many will reject God, and His plan of salvation. God has given people this choice, and they will reap the consequences of their choice. Many will choose to reject God plan for various reasons.

As teacher-leaders, it's important to understand that God works through us as we share His Word and our testimonies with others. Scripture tells us one plants, one waters, and one reaps, but it is God who gives the increase. A teacher-leader's responsibility is to do the best he/she can to obey God, pray for the students, prepare and present the lesson, keep order in the group meetings or classes, live the Christian life before God and others, and be an example for them. Though we all fall short, we should have a heart to give our best to God. If we do this, we have faithfully done our part.

A teacher-leader should never blame his/her self if the students choose not to commit their lives to Christ. God is sovereign, and able to cover us, even when we make big mistakes. We should never accept condemnation and think it's our fault when a person doesn't accept Christ. There can be as many reasons people fail to accept Christ as there are people who come up with those reasons. Here are a few I've heard:

1. God's not drawing them.

2. They aren't ready yet.

3. It's not God's time for them yet.

4. They don't have time because they're too busy.

5. They are distracted by other people, things, or circumstances in their lives.

6. They could be backslidden or prodigals who have walked away from God because they are unwilling to give up some besetting sin in their lives.

7. They could be angry with God, a church leader, or another Christian lay person because of a past experience, and that anger turned into bitterness. They aren't ready to give up their anger/bitterness, and return to God.

8. They are influenced by worldly people, and don't want to give up their sinful lifestyle to follow God.

Whatever is going on in the hearts and minds of the students may or may not become visible to the teacher-leader. If students decide not to share these things, we can't read their minds. At times, the Holy Spirit may give us insight, or a word to share with a student, or reveal the student's need to us. If this happens, we should obey the Holy Spirit, and share with the student. If the student doesn't open up, and we don't get revelation about the student from God, we should conduct our class or group as planned, and trust God for the results. He alone knows what's going on in the hearts and minds of our students.

At times a student will open up and share what's on their heart. If this happens, and the topic is appropriate for discussion in the class/group, take some time to listen. It could be God's opening the door for you to minister His word to the needs of the student. There have been many times God has used my teachings, testimonies, and personal experiences to help comfort or encourage others in need. This could be a divine appointment for you or someone in your class to help someone in need. Be open to the leading of the Holy Spirit, and follow His direction.

There are a few words of caution I would like to share:

1. Don't let someone monopolize your group time with all of their personal problems. Schedule a time when you can meet with them alone to share with them. If the personal problems are more than you can deal with, refer them to a Pastor or Christian counselor.

2. Tell your students that confidences shared in the group setting must not leave the room. These can easily turn to gossip, and people can get hurt. Be firm about this, and protect others from being hurt.

3. No one should be allowed to mock, ridicule, or tease another person with hurtful words. Your group environment should be a safe haven for people to share their hearts, and get help.

4. No person(s) should be allowed to turn your study group into a gab session about other things. Group time should be centered on sharing God's Word, and ministering to God's people. There are plenty of times, outside of group time, for people to visit with one another. In fact, you could even establish a fellowship time at the end of your Bible study, where people can meet, and visit with one another.

5. If you run into a problem with your class or group, remember—if you're a part of a church body—you have Pastors and church leaders who can help you with it. If you're not part of a church body, find someone, with experience in a church-leadership position, you can trust to give you good advice about handling your problem. If your problem is related to the Bible study, a church leader or Christian friend (who attends church), can help you find a solution to the situation, or refer you to a church leader.

May God richly bless you as you continue in your service to Him!

Your Guide Through the Lessons

This HEART to heart Bible Study provides you with twelve weekly lessons and a review activity. The lessons are comprised around a central theme. The review activity serves as the final lesson, and contains questions from all of the previous lessons. It will challenge the students to find the answers. They can use their study book as an aid.

Each lesson consists of sections, each with their own separate title, explaining the purpose for that part of the study. The titles of the sections—and their purposes—are listed below. There are no daily requirements, so the students can have flexibility, and complete the lesson according to their own schedules. Each one should be encouraged to study, reflect on God's word, and seek answers for their own personal lives. Also, the activities are made to encourage and challenge them to apply what they've learned to their life. The sections of each lesson are as follows:

Unit and Lesson Memory Verses

These are the verses listed directly under the title of the lesson. These verses present the main theme and topics of study. The Unit Verses are those listed in lesson one, because they give you the theme of the whole 13-week study. The other lessons' verses may only apply to that week's material. Everyone is encouraged to memorize these verses, as scripture memory empowers us so we can stand during the difficult times in our Christian walk. It also helps us to know if someone, who is sharing God's word with us, is speaking truth or not.

Beginning Activity

This activity provides you with an icebreaker, and gently nudges everyone to start thinking about the upcoming lesson. There will be a variety of activities to spark your interest.

Lesson Introduction

This section will introduce you to the lesson, and give you information and insight that may be needed before doing your weekly lesson.

In the Word

This is the main focus of the lesson. Whenever possible, students should read directly from the scripture to familiarize themselves with the Bible, and see the words for themselves. At times, the Scripture passages for the lesson may be paraphrased and shortened into a Bible story, because they include a wide range of chapters in the Bible, and it would be difficult to read, and include all of the material, in one weekly lesson.

Questions to Consider

These questions provide an opportunity for students to gain knowledge by studying God's word. Answering questions, and considering how they apply to your own personal life, will enrich your study, and increase your desire to learn God's word. Questions can also be great discussion starters!

Journal Activity

This activity provides students with an opportunity to meditate on what they've learned, and respond to the lesson. The activities are short and thought-provoking. Students are encouraged to think about the lesson, and how it can apply to their own personal lives. Studying God's Word without applying what you've learned will not yield much fruit.

Journal pages for each lesson are included in the back of the study book. So other than a pen or pencil and their Bible, students will not need to purchase more materials. The pages are for each student's personal use, and they can write down the journal activities, personal thoughts, ideas, questions, prayers, or anything else they desire. The students should never be required to share personal things they've written in their journals with others.

Everyone is encouraged to write something. It doesn't have to be long or perfect. This is not an English lesson, so there is no reason for anyone to struggle with the mechanics of writing. These activities are about learning the Bible, and letting God deal with your heart and life, and your thinking about and responding to His leading, and His word.

Decisions for Life

This section takes one or more points from the lesson, and brings them to the students on a personal level, asking, "What choice will you make for your life? Will you believe it or not? Will you apply what you've learned to your daily life?"

In Scripture the prophet Joel writes, "Multitudes, multitudes in the valley of decision! For the day of the Lord is near in the valley of decision." (Joel 3:14) As we learn God's Word, we make decisions that move us closer to spiritual life or spiritual death. I pray the students will choose life!

Life the Life

This activity provides the student with a choice of three or more activities which are designed to demonstrate how to put God's word into action in their daily walk with God. James 1:22 tells us, "But be doers of the word, and not hearers only, deceiving yourselves."

Review, Reflect, and Respond

This segment asks the student to review the lesson, reflect on what they've learned, and respond to it by writing out a brief paragraph about some part of it. This helps plant materials from the lesson into the hearts and minds of the students. The paragraphs can also be used as a reference, so they can periodically go back, look at their journal, and be reminded of the things they learned.

There are many ways to set up small group Bible studies. May God lead and guide you as you begin this journey, and *Behold Our Awesome God!*

Key Points in the Lessons

Below you will find a list of the lessons, and some of their key points. This list is not a complete list because the Holy Spirit could lead you to a question or topic other than the ones I've included in this guide. These are listed only to give you a starting point in the lesson. Begin here, and let the Holy Spirit lead you in the direction your group needs to go!

Lesson 1

1. God displays His awesome power to people everywhere.

2. God (Yahweh) is the only true God.

3. God can and will deliver His people from temptations, tests and trials, if that is His will.

4. If a law or command of a ruler goes against God's law, as believers, we are to obey God above earthly rulers.

Lesson 2

1. God works through His people to do awesome things.

2. God can and will provide for His people in every circumstance. God is all-sufficient and all we need.

3. God doesn't change. His miracles continue to be done each and every day.

4. God's miracles confirm the preaching and teaching of His word.

Lesson 3

1. God is omnipresent (everywhere present).

2. We can't hide or run away from God because He's always with us, and He knows where we are, and what we are doing.

3. God wants us to obey Him; it's proof of our love for Him. If we run or disobey, we may have to face hard consequences.

4. God will not change His mind about the tasks He wants us to do.

5. God values the soul of every person, even the wicked. They are more important to Him than temporal things—like Jonah's plant.

Lesson 4

1. God is big! He's too big to dwell in a temple made by human hands.

2. Though we make our plans, ultimately God will have the final say about them. However, God will not force anyone to love Him against their own will.

3. God knows the future, and He establishes rulers over the kingdoms.

4. God's dwelling place on earth today is in the hearts of His people—by faith—through the indwelling of the Holy Spirit.

5. We need to examine our perceptions of God to make sure we don't put Him in a small box—in our own minds—and limit His work in our lives.

Lesson 5

1. Our God is a personal God who wants relationship with each one of His people. He is not a God who is distant and doesn't want to interact with people. He wants interaction with us, and He wants to intervene in our lives, especially when we need His help!

2. God knows every detail about us and our lives, and He knew them all before He formed us in our mother's womb.

3. God sent Jesus to pay the penalty for our sin, and to be the way for us to be restored to fellowship with God, and for us to become adopted sons in God's kingdom, and His heavenly household.

4. God confronts us when we sin with a heart of love, and a motive of restoration. God doesn't want to judge or punish us. Our righteous God has to judge sin. Though God sometimes disciplines us; it's for our good, training, and restoration.

5. There may be consequences resulting from our sin that we may have to endure, even though God has forgiven us.

Lesson 6

1. God's nature is love.

2. Love is not self-seeking, but it sacrifices self for the betterment of others.

3. God demonstrated His love for us by sending Jesus to pay the penalty for our sins, and to be the way for us to become adopted

sons, and members of God's kingdom, and His heavenly household.

4. God commands us to love Him above all, and to love our neighbors as ourselves. By obeying these commands we demonstrate our love for God!

Lesson 7

1. God is three-in-one.

2. The three persons of the Godhead are: God the Father, The Holy Spirit, and Jesus—the Word in flesh—and only begotten Son of God. Together they make up one God.

3. The three persons of God are one—in agreement.

4. The three persons of God are working toward a single purpose—fulfilling God's plan and purpose in heaven, and on earth.

Lesson 8

1. God is our heavenly Father, the One who created us.

2. God is our Father through new birth (being born again) by the Holy Spirit.

3. The flesh gives birth to flesh; the Spirit gives birth to spirit.

4. We were created for God's pleasure, to have relationship with Him, and to praise and worship Him.

Lesson 9

1. God is Spirit; He is an invisible being.

2. Jesus used the wind to illustrate the working of the Holy Spirit.

3. You must be born again before you can see the kingdom of God, or understand God's word.

4. The Holy Spirit is the one that does the work of conversion in new birth.

5. Evidence of new birth is the change that takes place in a person's heart and life. God changes the person from the inside out, and the person desires the things of God, and gradually leaves the old nature and way of life behind. God transforms each person, but we will never be completely perfect until we go home to be with Him in heaven.

Lesson 10

1. God is the Word in flesh, the Son, Jesus.

2. Jesus is the fullness of the deity in human form.

3. Jesus came to earth to pay the penalty for our sins, and be the way for us to be saved, and become adopted sons in God's kingdom, and His heavenly household.

4. People can't work their way to heaven; one must be born again to enter the kingdom of God.

Lesson 11

1. God is "omniscient" meaning He knows everything.

2. God knows everything about each one of us.

3. Jesus is the Messiah who came to give eternal life.

4. God loves all people equally; there is no prejudice or favoritism in Him.

5. By sharing your testimony, God may use you to draw or convince others to believe in God.

Lesson 12

1. God is the Source of life.

2. God created all living creatures, and man and woman, and gave them life.

3. God created everything from nothing by speaking it into existence through the power of His word.

4. God has the power to overcome sickness and death, and to raise people from the dead.

Lesson 13

1. In the review activity, the students will review all of the characteristics of God, in one activity, to enhance the overall impact of the lessons. They will behold all of the attributes

of our awesome God in one weekly lesson, helping them to understand God is more awesome than we can ever fathom! No man or created being can ever be God.

2. God is awesome because of who He is!

3. God still does miracles, and He will not change.

4. God uses His people, working through them, to do awesome works! Works are done because we love God, not because we're trying to earn our way to heaven.

End notes

1   James, Susan (2002), *The Amazing Egg,* Compass Point Books, Minneapolis, Minnesota, U. S. A., pp. 10, 22.

2   Unger, Merrill F. (1957, 1961, 1966, 1967, 1969, 1970, 1971, 1972, 1973, 1974) *Unger's Bible Dictionary* (ISBN#0-8024-9035-2); Chicago: Moody Press, U. S. A., p. 1043.

3   Guralnik, David B., Editor, (1956, 1958, 1959, 1960, 1962, 1964, 1966, 1969, 1971) *Webster's New World Dictionary of the American Language with Student Handbook, Concise Edition,* Dictionary: World Publishing Company, New York, New York, U. S. A., Student Handbook: (1974), Southwestern Company, Nashville, Tennessee, U. S. A., p. 521.